GRAPHOLOGY

D1463785

Michael Watts
Illustrated by Gray Jolliffe

A Fireside Book
Published by Simon & Schuster
New York   London   Toronto   Sydney   Tokyo   Singapore

FIRESIDE
Simon & Schuster Building
Rockefeller Center
1230 Avenue of the Americas
New York, New York 10020

FIRESIDE and colophon are registered trademarks
of Simon & Schuster Inc.

Designed by Philip Mann, ACE Limited
Manufactured in the United States of America

1   3   5   7   9   10   8   6   4   2

Library of Congress Cataloging-in-Publication Data is available.

ISBN 0-671-78041-7

CONTENTS

Acknowledgements

Index

INTRODUCTION

When two people meet for the first time, they may shake hands and exchange polite verbal formalities, but underneath this visible ritual a more primal process is taking place. They are sizing one another up and classifying each other according to their own systems of measurement, part of a 'survival' response bent on assessing possible future friendship or the opportunity to dominate, a genetic programme that extends throughout most of the animal kingdom. Dog owners know how their pet, on meeting another dog, frequently heads straight for its tail in order to sniff out the character. Fortunately graphology offers a far more socially acceptable means of determining someone's true personality.

Since writing is a pattern of movements produced by the mind, it isn't really surprising that it can yield so much information about a human being. Although the hand manipulates the pen, it is the brain which is in control, for it is the brain which conceives the thoughts, feelings and ideas contained in the writing, and the hand of the individual is simply the most convenient vehicle it can use to record its message on paper.

Psychologists, as well as others in professions such as the police and personnel recruitment, have long recognised that people demonstrate many aspects of personality through the silent yet expressive language of their bodies. Small, perhaps hardly noticeable movements of the eyes and facial features, as well as larger, more obvious gestures of the hands and other body parts, can shed far more light on a person's personality than the words that a person speaks. It is interesting to note that the most subtle movements are often the most revealing – a minute shifting of someone's eyes accompanying their spoken words can, for instance, make it clear to the trained observer that a person is lying. In general, the smaller the body movement, the more reliable it is as a source of information, because tiny movements are exceptionally difficult to control.

Handwriting is an excellent display of very subtle expressive movements and is therefore one of the most valid means of detecting character. Writing also offers the most practical opportunity for interpreting expressive gestures, for it is 'frozen movement' – it captures and holds, in visible form, even the slightest and most subtle motions which can then be studied and interpreted long after the movements have been produced. With graphology, much that is hidden, latent or suppressed in a personality may come to light on a single sheet of paper. Another principal quality is that it is non-discriminatory and cannot therefore be misused by the prejudiced mind.

If graphology – the study of handwriting – is such an effective means of detecting human nature, why has there not been considerably more scientific research into this system? Why has it taken so long for it to gain any real recognition?

The answer is clear – before this century only the most educated people in society could read and write; the average person was invariably illiterate. Consequently there was little motivation to study handwriting analysis for at best it would provide a means of assessing personality that could only be used on an extremely limited section of the population. There are no reliable known records which show exactly when the development of handwriting analysis began, though statements attributed to Aristotle suggest that he was sensitive to the connection between a man's writing and his character. But it was not until 1622, shortly after the invention in the West of the printing press, that the first known book on the subject was published.

This was a short book written by an Italian scholar, Camille Baldo, and it did little more than gather dust: it was written in a style that would have been all but incomprehensible even to the interested. However, in the latter part of the nineteenth century a French clergyman, Abbé Jean-Hippolyte Michons of Paris, was introduced to the idea of handwriting analysis by Baldo's book. He carried out his own research and in 1872 published the first popular book in this field, creating the word 'graphology' to describe it. He is considered the father of graphology as we know it.

Since that time the field of research has widened and in universities in Switzerland, Germany, France, Israel and other countries graphology is now included as part of degree courses in Psychology. Although it is far from being an exact science, graphology is now based on over a century of empirical research and today, in the hands of a competent operator, results are remarkably accurate. Many major corporations have been using graphology in personnel selection for the last fifty years.

This book on handwriting analysis is uniquely based upon the following insight. I have always found that although a human being has an abundance of different characteristics which add together to form the total personality, it is only the really strong dominant characteristics which significantly influence behaviour, and these will be very few in number. So in a piece of handwriting containing, say, sixty identifiable writing features, only a few dominant ones, perhaps five or six, will play an essential role in revealing the person's actual behaviour and personality. The remaining 'minor' features should be ignored, as they will exert only an insignificant influence over behaviour and if taken into account may confuse matters.

Many books on graphology present a wealth of information and theory that in practice is entirely unusable, and therefore extremely frustrating, as it tends to sap the reader's self-confidence by 'mystifying' graphology and keeping it in esoteric realms.

In this book the essential elements are clearly set out in a practical, usable way and can be immediately, and almost effortlessly, applied to give astonishing results: the reader will be able to analyse writing effectively almost from the start. Spotting the dominant features in a writing sample is made easy by the clear examples of handwriting given in each chapter, as well as in the index, so there is no room whatsoever for doubt. Because the important features stand out so clearly, it becomes unnecessary to carry on one's person the list of tools recommended by most graphologists – magnifying glass, protractor, ruler marked in millimetres, etc. As so often in life, it is the less complicated approach which yields the most satisfying results.

I have not used graphological terminology, which is of interest to and used only by the dedicated handwriting analyst, nor will it be necessary to have read and assimilated information from earlier chapters in order to make sense of the examples on any particular page. The reader will be able to begin analysing a piece of handwriting immediately. I *have* used one term – 'the central zone' – frequently: this refers to the central section of writing containing letters such as 'm', 'n', 's', 'o' etc as well as portions of any other letters which occupy the same area.

This book begins with a concise description of the nature of the ego, the main foundation stone of most personality characteristics, followed by a description of the two extreme expressions of the ego, the small ego and the big ego. The rest of the chapters are mostly double-page spreads, mini-portraits of personality characteristics, together with the different letter shapes and writing features that reveal them. These are shown in each chapter under the heading 'Signs to look for'. A given letter shape will apply to writing of any size or style, whether it is neat or not, easily legible or not. Sometimes you will be required to spot a particular sign several times in the writing in order to be sure of the corresponding aspect of personality. I have not devoted a chapter exclusively to signatures as those which can be interpreted with accuracy are described with clear examples in the appropriate chapters. The index will also provide you with examples of these signatures, together with their relevant page numbers.

It should now be obvious that this book's method of handwriting analysis is incredibly simple as well as soundly based. But what exactly do you stand to gain from it?

You will achieve a deeper understanding of yourself and your real potentials and this will assist you in making the correct choices for your life. In addition, you will learn much about the true personality of friends, family and work associates – the social mask that others adopt will no longer hide them from your view. Even the personality of deceased relatives, whom you barely remember or never met, will no longer remain a mystery, provided that you have a piece of their handwriting. Possibly most important of all, this book can be of very great use in revealing what any prospective partner is really going to be like to live or work with. Any relationship can prove difficult, but a significant contributing factor is the mutual deception with which it may begin.

When we meet someone with whom we want to start a relationship, what we like about them is the censored version of that person, the costume they don to play their chosen role. They also fall into the same trap about us. After a while the real selves emerge and may be totally incompatible, though the personalities of the original roles may have been perfectly suited. Using a knowledge of handwriting analysis, such mistakes can be avoided. All you need is half a page or more of someone's normal handwriting (not a hurried, scribbled note) together with their signature, written with a pen of their choice while they are seated comfortably at a table or desk, and you're ready to start using this book now.

It doesn't matter what the writing is about. If someone seems unable to think of anything to write for you, suggest they describe what they have been doing that day or, as a last resort, give them the following sentence to write, which contains all the letters of the alphabet: *I thought I saw the quick brown fox jumping over the lazy doggy – I looked again and then saw it was only foggy*. Handwriting samples written under the influence of alcohol, drugs, severe fatigue or illness are not eligible.

The contents list will give you the page number of any aspect of a person that interests you and that chapter will provide a description of the personality characteristics as well as clear examples of handwriting signs that disclose it. Alternatively, the index will give you quick references to pages explaining the meaning of different letter shapes and aspects of writing style that you are looking at. You don't need to begin with the first, general chapter. This book is specially geared to suit all types of readers, including the impatient sort who may prefer to dive straight into the middle of the book or any other place that captures their attention. To avoid awkward phrasing or repetition, **and for no other reason**, the personal pronoun 'he' has been used, although the material in each chapter applies equally to men and women unless otherwise specified.

Now you're ready to begin the fun of exploration but before you do so please remember to use the information presented here with sensitivity and discretion.

Graphology has the potential to expand your knowledge of human personality considerably. But knowledge is a power which can be used both positively and negatively and the knowledge gained from this book should never be used as a weapon to hurt or criticise.

If you want to develop your skills in graphology, practice is obviously indispensable, so whenever someone is willing to let you look at their handwriting, don't pass up the opportunity (most people are pleased you are interested in them and are highly inquisitive to know your results). A word of warning, however. You may at times uncover a personality characteristic that you feel can't be right as there is no outward sign of it. There are three possible explanations for this. First, you may simply not know the person well enough to judge. Secondly, if the person is aware of this characteristic and considers it undesirable he may have been able to inhibit its expression (a human being can potentially free himself from the influence of most behaviour patterns, if his wish is strong enough). Alternatively, the characteristic may exist in his behaviour but will be concealed from all but those who are exceptionally close to him. Then again, handwriting is affected by mood and energy level at the time of writing; this could exaggerate certain aspects of it or throw up apparently contradictory signs.

There is another important factor to consider which other books on graphology do not explain. Personalities are complex, so one particular characteristic may manifest itself in different ways with different people, interacting with other qualities. For instance, someone interested in money may not display the expected handwriting signs but may instead display traits that reveal a love of attention – money is not an end in itself, merely a means chosen to achieve 'celebrity status'. To give other examples: someone who is a good mechanic may not show 'The Mechanical Mind' chapter's writing signs but may instead show those featured for 'The Analytical Mind'; someone known to be jealous may not show up as that but as 'fault-finding'.

Respect the feelings and privacy of the person you are analysing by not telling them about their personality in front of other people, unless they specifically ask you to do so. In a one-to-one talk you are in a position to be more open and, if requested, can more freely discuss the less desirable aspects of their behaviour without causing embarrassment. Above all, use tact and learn to sense a person's emotional response to what you are saying. Sometimes things you see in writing are better left unsaid, though you will be the wiser for spotting them. If you do discover something about yourself or someone else that you feel cannot be true, remember to check that your interpretation and judgement have not been influenced by preconceived ideas, whether about yourself or anyone else. You have to be objective to get the best out of graphology.

And now – begin!

THE EGO

For the moment, think of your ego as an independent-minded little creature who has set up a place of permanent residence in your brain. Its character and behaviour have been shaped by all your life experiences up till now.

The ego is an outward expression of our inner will to survive and to make our mark as a separate individual. Most people identify so closely with their ego that they believe it to be the sum-total of who they are, failing to realise that this set of conditioned behaviour patterns is simply a part of, and not the whole of their total being.

The size of our handwriting can reveal a great deal about our personality and is a major feature used in determining how much power and personal recognition our ego is demanding.

The Small Ego

Just as a magnifying glass can focus energy from the sun to form a single point of burning intensity, so the individual with Very Small Writing is able to focus full attention single-mindedly on one thing at a time, possessing the valuable gift of concentration. Consequently, the faculties of his intellect operate at a high level of efficiency. The powerful beam of his attention brightly illuminates all it touches, engraving deeply etched, crystal-clear images in the memory centres of the brain. He remembers minute details of specific incidents that took place even in early childhood.

In his chosen field of employment, his effortless recall of essential facts will be an undeniable asset. He will be suited to work requiring close attention to small details and may well be adept at using his hands to perform fine movements needing a high degree of precision. In a career compatible with his abilities, he will be self-disciplined, reliable and very hardworking.

Socially, this person will tend to have very few close friends. He greatly values his privacy and feels ill at ease in situations such as parties, which often require superficial contact with a lot of people, though he may have learnt to hide these inner feelings with a display of self-confidence.

Because he has a mind that automatically notices small details, this may cause him at times to be somewhat petty and pedantic in intimate relationships – unnecessarily fussy and over-concerned with the significance of trivial matters. Partners should also be aware that this person cannot handle the direct emotional confrontation of full-blown argument. Instead, he will make a hasty retreat and may express anger silently by indulging in an extended sulking session or becoming emotionally withdrawn in the private world of his own mind.

It is highly probable that such behaviour stems from a pressured and stressful childhood which suppressed emotional expression and weakened self-esteem. Unpleasant school experiences may have contributed to this, but the major factor is likely to have been a parent with a forceful, domineering and judgemental nature.

The individual with very small writing is very conscious of what others on this planet have accomplished and sets his own life in this perspective. With his way of viewing the world, he is able to find only very short-lived satisfaction from any successes and will rarely, if ever, have moments when he feels he has 'arrived'. One famous person with very small writing was the scientist, Albert Einstein. He once described his work as no more significant than a single grain of sand on a beach. But then, he was viewing what he had achieved in relation to the infinite universe.

In some cases, people who have writing which reveals a small ego will mask their true nature, usually for reasons of ambition, by adopting a façade which gives the totally opposite impression.

Signs to look for: handwriting **of any style** that satisfies this point:

1 Writing with the central zone as small or smaller than this:

The Big Ego

Very Large Writing occupies a great deal of space on paper and, similarly, a person with this writing characteristic has an ego which needs and expects a lot out of his life in order to find some degree of satisfaction; indeed a major motivating force which rules much of his behaviour comes from a relentless desire to gain a position of distinction. He yearns strongly to be admired and respected, and shines when he is the centre of attention.

The person with large writing is almost always self-reliant and a highly independent thinker with plenty of initiative. Consequently, there could well be friction with superiors as he strongly resents authority imposing restrictions. He needs freedom to work in an independent manner and if given this is likely to be an optimistic, determined and enterprising employee with progressive ideas and plenty of ambition. He will, however, be unlikely to tolerate any form of work he considers monotonous or routine: he needs interest and variety to stimulate his motivation. He will tend to voice his opinions openly and needs to be careful not to appear tactless or conceited in doing so. He is most definitely best suited to careers offering plenty of contact with other people: working in isolation would not provide opportunities to elicit the social recognition he requires for the sustenance of his self-esteem. There are a few exceptions to this: in the literary or artistic professions, isolation would be compensated by the public display of a finished product worthy of appreciation.

In social settings he is in his element, for large writing is a clear indication of an extrovert. He will have a strong presence, with plenty of self-assurance and poise, the sort of person who will always stand out in a crowd or party, vivacious and enthusiastic, his conversation entertaining. Undoubtedly he will be something of an exhibitionist.

If you are intending to begin an intimate relationship with him, don't expect your existence to be all fun and games. Though you will rarely be bored living with such a colourful, animated personality, you are bound to have some very stormy times unless you keep in mind that it is well worth the effort to supply him frequently with genuine praise and admiration: he will respond to this treatment with an abundance of good vibrations, for he is capable of being extremely generous and warm-hearted. Dare to criticise him, however, and you will have to bear the inevitable disastrous consequences. Reach mutual agreement as soon as possible as to how you are going to share decision-making or his assertive, headstrong personality will claim more than his fair share of control and you'll end up living with a benevolent dictator.

The child-like part of human nature plays its most active role in the character of a person with large writing. At times his playful, enthusiastic and often spontaneous manner can be irresistibly attractive. He has the enviable capacity at times to enjoy the moment to the full, with no thought of tomorrow. The other side of this child-like nature will inevitably surface and you will come face to face with an egocentric, temperamental spoilt brat who can completely lose sight of objectivity and blow up trivial occurrences out of all proportion. But at the end of the day, in spite of his sizeable portion of failings, he can be a great person to have around, for his fun-loving nature will be a frequent entertainment and if you touch his heartstrings, he can be amongst the most loving of partners.

Signs to look for: handwriting **of any style** that satisfies this point:

1 Writing with the central zone as large or larger than this:

CENTRAL ZONE

AMBITION

Ambition is the desire to achieve more. The quality and type of ambition an individual possesses is determined both genetically (by innate physical energy, fighting instinct, etc) and by other influences (country, family values, school, etc). The presence or lack of ambition in a personality probably has more influence in shaping a person's destiny than any other single factor.

We not only have an ego, formed by our life experiences and influencing the perception we have of our personality, possessions and achievements. We also have an ideal ego, a picture of who we would like to be, which is also defined in terms of personality, possessions and achievements.

A person with only a small difference between his ego and his ideal ego will invariably be an under-achiever without much ambition, but because he makes little use of his potential he will inevitably feel unfulfilled. The individual with a massive difference between his ego and his ideal ego will be ruled and obsessed by excessive ambition, destined to be eternally frustrated in his attempts to achieve the unreachable. He fools himself into believing that when he reaches a certain point he will be satisfied but this is never the case, for his goals, if approached, are immediately redefined so that however far he progresses, the gap between where he is and where he wishes to be remains unchanged.

In between these two extremes are a collection of characters you may meet any day of the week and which are among the most outwardly recognisable types. If you're in doubt, you'll soon detect them from the clues in their writing.

Leaders

Such people will be very frustrated and unfulfilled if not employed in a position of responsibility and authority, for they have a strong inner desire to direct others and will feel a failure unless they do so: taking orders causes them considerable stress. In a personal relationship, a leader will obviously have conflicts with a partner of the same temperament. In such circumstances mutual agreement will have to be reached as to how responsibilities will be shared, so that there is no competition for control. With a passive partner, this individual will dominate a large portion of their relationship, at times to excess.

Signs to look for: handwriting **of any style** that satisfies one or more of these points:

1 Capital or small letters with a final line rising noticeably higher and that curves to the right or stays vertical (you need to find 2 or more letters like this).

H H N N V V W W v v w

2 Capital or small letters beginning with a rigid diagonal line starting from noticeably below the central zone (look for 2 or more letters starting this way).

M M a b g him o s w ← CENTRAL ZONE

3 The small letter 'g' or 'y' with a sharply angled triangle **of any shape** (watch for 2 or more triangles like this).

g g g g g y y y y

4 The small, angular letter 'm' in writing where heavy pen pressure makes indentations that clearly show on the reverse of the paper (spot 4 or more 'm's where this applies). Note the sharp angles at top and bottom.

man met mud him map

5 The capital or small letter 't' with the crossbar sloping upwards or downwards (you will need to find 4 or more 't's like this to be sure this applies).

Tim toy Tom Top too tin it to toy

6 The capital or small letter 't' with a crossbar at least twice as long as the stem (check that you spot 4 or more 't's with this).

Tea Tom too tip it

7 Handwriting where the central zone is as large or larger than this:

dog many big you landing in

CENTRAL ZONE

The Perfectionist

This person is extremely alert and observant, has good concentration, plenty of mental stamina and a reliable memory for facts. He is conscientious and extremely punctual, someone who requires his work to meet the highest possible standards – anything less than his best is unacceptable and will cause him to be markedly self-critical. He is the type of person who keeps well-ordered files recording all his transactions and who, when required to present written reports, can be relied upon never to omit any essentials – he takes pride in a job well done. He has an uncanny eye for detail, which he meticulously registers before making any judgements: you can be sure he will scrutinise all the fine print before putting his signature on any legal documents. He does, however, need to make sure that this obsession with detail does not result in his spending a disproportionate amount of available time on the less significant aspects of a job at the expense of what is really important.

His partner could well find him irritatingly fussy and pedantic: he is one of those people who immediately notice a crumb on the floor or a failure to put something in its proper place. Any form of slovenliness or absentmindedness or a disorganised environment at home will be intolerable to him, for he is a naturally fastidious person who needs everything to be 'just so' in order to relax.

Signs to look for: handwriting **of any style** that satisfies one or more of these points:

1 Rigidly straight lines of handwriting on unruled paper that appear to have been written with the help of a ruler.

glad you could come   this is just fine

2 The small letter 'i' with the dot nearly always very close to and directly above the stem.

if it is interesting   it isnt difficult is it ?

3 The small letter 't' with the stem nearly always passing through the exact centre of the crossbar.

that is the time to try to state that fact

4 Handwriting neatly framed by wide, even margins on all four sides.

D.LIGHT
HIGH RD
LONDON
N.W.11

Dear Sue,
        just enter
the stillness of your
"inner being" which is
pure consciousness.
        We are all part
of that endless ocean
of Universal Energy
called Love
        Dave

The Artist
of Life
lives in
the moment
free as
the Wind

5 Writing composed entirely of precisely formed capital letters of uniform size, with evenly spaced words in straight lines.

LET IT BE AND TAKE IT EASY   BE HERE NOW !

The Attention Grabber

These people crave admiration and respect and simply thrive on being noticed at social gatherings, for their self-esteem relies strongly on recognition and without it will weaken rapidly.

They invariably seek employment in areas which put them in the public eye or in a position where colleagues look up to them. They have a self-assured manner and will try to be entertaining and lively in conversation. Without doubt they have extrovert tendencies but you can be sure they will work hard in any job which satisfies the ego's needs.

In intimate relationships, any kind of compliment will be music to their ears.

Signs to look for: handwriting **of any style** that satisfies one or more of these points:

1 Any signature that is quite obviously large or showy.

Bob Finlay   Jim Mills   Chad Hill

2 Any signature underlined by more than one line or by a single line that is wavy or elaborate.

Dan Foe   Mhula   Tom King   Shirley Anne

3 Capital letters in handwriting or signature at least 3½ times the size of the central zone (you will need to find 2 or more letters like this).

Robert Smith   Dear mum

4 Handwriting with the central zone as large or larger than this:

dog many big you landing in

CENTRAL ZONE

The Workaholic

This person is likely to have good stamina – the sort who is always prepared to work round the clock to get things done, who sets his mind on achieving something and if his energy level gets low, simply uses his willpower to override any warning signals which indicate he is placing himself under too much physical or emotional stress.

His partner is likely to find that he pays her little attention and that he is at times somewhat irritable and impatient because he is constantly stressed. In most cases, the workaholic is compulsively driven by deeply rooted fears and anxieties, such as financial insecurity, inadequacy in close emotional relationships or excessive concern with maintaining social status.

Signs to look for: handwriting **of any style** that satisfies one or more of these points:

1 Illegibility of letters in many words caused by fast writing.

2 The small letter 'g' or 'y' with the descending line appearing to be pulled to the right (look for 3 or more letters that do this).

3 The small letter 'g' with a descending line at least 4½ times the size of the central zone (spot 3 or more letters where this applies).

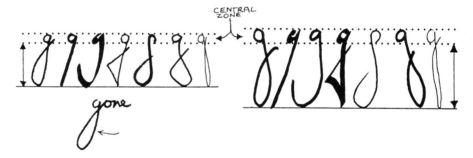

4 The small letter 't' with the crossbar on the right detached from the stem in writing where the central zone is as small or smaller than this (you will need to see 2 or more 't's like this).

The Hedonist

This person is determined to succeed in his career, to satisfy an insatiable desire to live life to the full and to enjoy the luxuries and comforts that success and money can bring. He has a strong sensual nature combined with an abundance of vitality. Someone whose handwriting includes the graphological sign described in point 4, denoting a strong force of natural animal instinct, could be inclined to lash out when angered. Self-denial is quite alien to the hedonist – he would rather have his fun now and pay later. He must be careful, though, because his inclinations predispose him to over-indulge and he may dissipate a great deal of life energy, and precipitate ill health, by eating and drinking to excess.

To help avoid this destructive way of living he would be well advised to exploit his innate capacity to savour the beauty of Nature, for he is ruled by instinct more than most and his senses will be easily stimulated by natural pleasures of outdoor life, even if his usual lifestyle tends to deny this. He will feel very frustrated if his partner does not share his love of pleasure, for he quite definitely harmonises best with fellow hedonists like himself.

Signs to look for: handwriting **of any style** that satisfies **two** or more of these points:

1 Writing done from choice with a medium or thick felt-tip pen, or any other pen producing broad thick lines.

Relaxation **feelings** *Awareness*

2 One or more of the following letter shapes appearing in the writing at least twice:

The small letter 'd' where the stem is a single ascending line curving to the left

dog grade day dim lic **mud**

The capital or small letter 'e' shaped like a backward-facing number 3

Edna *egg meal Easy pet End*

The capital or small letter 'f' shaped like a treble clef

felicity fat f far drift for

The small letter 'g' shaped like a number 8 or an elongated letter 's'. The 'g' must be the first letter in a word to be valid.

gone **got gum** *give grill glad*

3 The small letter 'g' with an over-inflated balloon appearance **of any shape** (you will need to find 4 or more 'g's like this).

g g g g g g

4 Any letters clogged with ink (you must find 4 or more letters like this).

what is that Come back look at it

23

The Fighter

This individual is always on the alert, ready to tackle any obstacle he encounters on the road to achieving his ambitions. His competitive nature and natural fighting spirit generate a strong urge to win, supported by a great deal of determination and an in-built resilience to setbacks. He never loses heart for long and when he really sets his mind on something he won't give up till he succeeds, pursuing his objectives with great intensity and little hesitation. His enjoyment of new challenges enables him to work long hours and if he feels he has the potential he will push hard to be one of the best in his field. Equally, if he has a tendency towards over-indulgence, he can be adversely influenced by friends with destructive habits, such as smoking or excessive drinking, for his competitive nature may lead him to be the worst of the lot.

He will at times be difficult to live with because he is always prepared to argue and rarely gives in to apologise first. On the positive side, he is likely to be someone who would fearlessly protect a loved one in the face of danger and can be relied upon to cope successfully in situations that call for the survival instinct.

Signs to look for: handwriting **of any style** that satisfies one or more of these points:

1 The small letters 'h', 'm' **and** 'n' sharply angled at top and bottom (you must spot 4 or more letters **of each** letter where this applies).

2 The small letter 'g' or 'y' with a sharply angled triangle **of any shape** (watch for 2 or more triangles like this).

3 Capital or small letters with a final line rising noticeably higher and curving to the right (look for 2 or more letters where this applies).

4 The small letter 'm' or 'n' shaped like a shark's tooth (you need to see 2 or more letters like this).

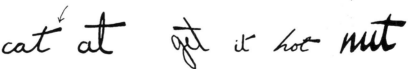

5 The small letter 't' with a crossbar that **noticeably thickens** on one side (look for 2 or more 't's where this applies).

6 Capital or small letters with a hook or hooks (you will need to find 4 or more letters like this).

7 Writing where heavy pen pressure makes indentations that show clearly on the reverse of the paper.

The Money Lover

This person's favourite activity will be cooking up some financial scheme. Aware that wealth brings status and power, his self-esteem is directly related to how well he has achieved financially. Generally, his powerful desire for money will ensure he is fairly well-off, materially. He will only consider jobs that offer good financial opportunities, but will be highly motivated and will work long hours. He will be a good provider, prepared to make sacrifices in his pursuit of wealth. He will want a stable partner able to manage the household budget rather than a romantic idealist content to live in rags and poverty.

Signs to look for: handwriting **of any style** that satisfies either or both of these points:

1 The small letter 'y' with a descending line at least 3½ times the size of the central zone (find 3 or more 'y's with the descending line this long).

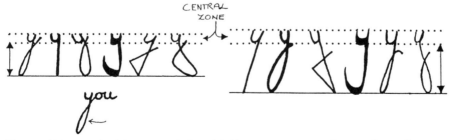

2 The small letter 'y' with an over-inflated balloon appearance **of any shape** (you must spot 3 or more 'y's like this).

MINDPOWER

Is the way you think fast, slow, logical, intuitive, analytical, creative, investigative, independent, flexible? The answer to this question is of extreme importance, for the way we think really does shape the course of our destiny and determine our level of happiness.

Developing a positive and intelligent way of thinking is the fundamental aim of almost all self-improvement techniques, ranging from conventional psychotherapy in the West to the more esoteric disciplines of the East. Now you can find out how your own mind works and expresses itself, and how other people display their attitudes to life.

The Literary Type

This individual has a strong sense of culture, a love of good literature and an unmistakable flair for words. He is capable of writing professionally and with his skilful command of language will have no trouble articulating thoughts and feelings, or concisely relating factual information. He will obviously most enjoy working in journalism, advertising, publishing, etc, and given the motivation and opportunity could well derive great satisfaction as an author. He has a good intellect, a cultivated mind and appreciates interesting discussions and all the finer things in life.

Signs to look for: handwriting **of any style** containing 'the literary g' or **three** or more of the other points:

The literary g
The small letter 'g' shaped like a number 8 or an elongated letter 's'. The 'g' must be the first letter of a word to be valid (make sure you see 3 or more 'g's like this).

gone got gum give grill glad

1 The small letter 'd' where the stem is a single ascending line that curves to the left or right or stays vertical (look for 2 or more 'd's where this applies).

dog nod day grade hid lie dim

2 The capital or small letter 'e' shaped like a backward-facing number 3 (spot 2 or more 'e's made this way).

Edna egg meal Easy pet End

28

3 The capital or small letter 'f' shaped like a treble clef (you need to find 2 or more 'f's like this).

felicity fat & far drift for

4 The capital or small letter 'm' like 2 or 3 joined letter 'i's without dots (make certain you see 3 or more 'm's like this).

iiet naiiie Mary home my Man

5 The capital or small letter 't' with the crossbar sharp like a needlepoint on either side (watch for 3 or more 't's that do this).

at met kool try tea Tom bet

6 The capital or small letter 't' where the crossbar forms part of the following letter 'h' (you must see 3 or more 't's where this applies).

The Thanks the with this them

The Free Spirit

This person usually prefers to sort out and solve his problems alone, disliking any interference or unsolicited assistance. His goals are self-made and he maps out his own destiny in life, uninfluenced by the expectations others may have of him. His resolve will not be weakened by negative criticism, for he is fairly strong-minded and will usually dismiss unpleasant vibrations with a shrug. He refuses to accept blindly the established ways of doing and thinking, and will always examine the validity of rules and regulations imposed on him, questioning any restrictions which seem unjust or which threaten his individuality.

At work he is always willing to cut through any unnecessary red tape, ignoring tradition and set procedures which he considers obstacles to progress. He is not well suited to employment which calls for group effort and which suppresses individual resourcefulness. His work environment must be one which allows him freedom to act and think independently, otherwise he is destined to have conflicts with the boss and, if pushed too far, will be openly hostile.

Signs to look for: handwriting **of any style** that satisfies one or more of these points:

1 Any signature underlined by a single line detached from the signature.

2 The small letter 'd' with the stem **not more than** 1½ times the size of the central zone (be sure you see 4 or more 'd's like this).

3 The small letter 't' with the stem **not more than** 1½ times the size of the central zone (look for 4 or more 't's this size).

The Mechanical Mind

This person has the potential to achieve a high level of proficiency in jobs of a technical nature demanding a significant degree of manual dexterity. He has a natural aptitude for performing fine, precision movements requiring attention to detail. He will have a well above average capacity to develop an understanding of how machinery operates and an innate feel for structure.

His best chance in finding career satisfaction and success lies in choosing a job in fields such as electronics, mechanics, engineering, graphic design, interior design, architecture, clothes design or the building industry. Secretaries with this quality frequently seem to have exceptional shorthand and typing skills. If his career does not involve any of these areas he might use his talents by being handy with do-it-yourself jobs in the home or may express himself through creative hobbies, such as painting or gardening.

Signs to look for: handwriting **of any style** that satisfies one or more of these points:

1 Writing composed entirely or almost entirely of capital letters.

GREAT IDEA! IT LOOKS FINE FEELING GOOD

2 The small letter 'm' with flat, level tops (spot 2 or more 'm's like this).

game dream machine mixing

3 The small letter 'n' with a flat, level top (check you have 2 or more 'n's of this sort).

gun tin handle new name

4 The small letter 'm' with rounded, level tops (find 4 or more 'm's like this).

many main am MIX most my

5 The small letter 'r' with a flat top (look for 2 or more 'r's with this flat top).

are cream reality alarm

6 The small letter 'r' with two peaks (you will need 4 or more 'r's like this).

heart Create drift army

7 Any letters joined to the next letter by a **straight** horizontal line (you must find 3 or more letters that do this).

bat fun vividly warm good

The Intuitive Type

This person often finds solutions to problems instantly without having to use the more time-consuming conscious processes of methodical reasoning and analysis – he has the gift of intuition, of quick perception of the truth without apparent effort. It is as though he has a sixth sense. In emergencies this faculty will be a tremendous asset – he will react instinctively, without delay, to potential dangers. He is also capable of perceiving another person's feelings very accurately, as well as his own – he will tend to make immediate decisions about whether or not he likes someone when he meets them for the first time. Sometimes he experiences unexplained gut feelings, messages from the subconscious mind, about a person or situation, which he cannot justify logically but which he still feels convinced he can trust.

It is clear that this individual has direct access to a most valuable human ability. Indeed, Einstein and other scientific pioneers have stated their belief that intuition is potentially far superior to logic as it plumbs all the information in the subconscious mind, whereas logic relies on information-processing based only on thoughts occurring at a conscious level of awareness. In the tradition of Japanese Zen Buddhism, and in many of the martial arts, an intuitive level of consciousness (known in Japan as *mushin*) is considered the pinnacle of human achievement and therefore the ultimate goal of inner development.

Signs to look for: handwriting **of any style** that satisfies **two** or more of these points:

1 The small letter 'g' shaped like a number 8 or an elongated letter 's'. The 'g' must be the first letter in a word to be valid (check that you see 3 or more 'g's like this).

gone got gum give grill glad

2 The capital or small letter 'm' like 2 or 3 joined letter 'i's without dots (you will need to see 4 or more 'm's made this way).

iiet naiiie Mary home my Man

3 Writing with many words having a mixture of letters joined to each other, and gaps between some letters that could have been joined up. Gaps caused by breaking off to dot 'i's, cross 't's or place apostrophes are not valid.

remember always the moment Silence is Creative

The Logical Thinker

This person has developed an unshakable faith in his own powers of observation and deduction, and when expressing his views will do so step by step with an air of certainty which will inspire others to have confidence in him. In his chosen career, he will inevitably be respected for his sound judgement and reliable professional knowledge. In social situations, those looking for intelligent, intellectual discussions will find him a stimulating conversationalist and a good listener, who will show great respect for any opinions presented to him which are based on sound reasoning. He is unlikely to have much time for those he considers irrational.

If he is involved in an intimate relationship with an emotional, intuitive partner, he may at times appear somewhat insensitive, as he will have great difficulty in understanding or accepting the mystery of her instinctive behaviour. On the other hand, his partner can rest assured that should he become irritable she will have a very good chance of appeasing him by appealing to his sense of reason.

The following description will only apply when all the letters are fully connected in all the words of the handwriting sample, with no exceptions: because he has seen the effectiveness of logic from numerous past experiences, it has become something of a security blanket to him which he cannot relinquish at any cost. It forms the roots of his intellectual and professional self-confidence, which he possesses in abundance. It means that he will not trust intuition in himself or others.

Signs to look for: handwriting **of any style** that satisfies one or more of these points:

1 Writing in which almost every word has its letters fully joined together except for gaps caused by breaking off to dot 'i's, cross 't's or place apostrophes.

finding the way   Keeping a positive attitude

2 Writing in which almost every word has its letters fully joined together,

everything changing   letting the past go by

3 Any word joined by a line to the next word (you must find 3 or more words joined in this way).

are you sure? I could have   Nice and easy

The Inquisitive Type

NB See also The Analytical Mind

This individual is likely to have a clear, systematic way of thinking and a sceptical attitude towards any new ideas unless he sees that they are grounded on solid facts. He also has a naturally enquiring mind that generates a desire to learn and to discover for himself. He is open to exploring new ways of finding solutions to problems: he certainly does not appreciate mundane, routine work. Potentially useful information is subjected to intense analysis from every possible angle. He welcomes challenges and when he sets his sights on achieving a desired goal, he is fuelled by a strong, unhesitating determination and pursues his objectives single-mindedly. The brain of such a person is rarely quiet and he will frequently at night find himself restlessly contemplating the activities of the day, and this could well make it difficult for him to get to sleep.

Signs to look for: handwriting **of any style** that satisfies either or both of these points:

1 The small letter 'm' sharply angled at top and bottom (look for 4 or more 'm's like this).

man   met   mud   him   map

2 The small letter 'r' with two peaks – the first **must be** noticeably taller (you will need to find 4 or more 'r's with this).

water   rest   early   letters   heart

T h e   S u p e r   M e m o r y

This person closely observes even small details and because his attention is so concentrated, it retains lasting impressions, even from as far back as early childhood.

This is of tremendous value to him in any work that involves tasks requiring accurate assimilation and permanent retention of a great deal of new information. His approach to such jobs will be organised, methodical and extremely efficient, even though he may take a reasonable amount of time to memorise material. For any information relating to his subjects or hobbies, you can put away your encyclopaedia and trust him to be an authority.

Signs to look for: handwriting **of any style** that satisfies one or more of these points:

1 The small letter 'i' with the dot very close to and directly above the stem (be sure you 4 or more 'i's with the dot in this position).

if it is interesting it isnt difficult is it ?

2 The small letter 'i' with the dot **nearly always** directly above the stem (though not necessarily close to it).

it is limiting this idea is original

3 Handwriting where the central zone is as small or smaller than this:

along something regarding anything surprising thing interesting

CENTRAL ZONE

The Quick Thinker

His mind seems to function without any apparent conscious mental effort; at work you can expect him to be the sort who can size up situations at a glance and respond with snap decisions. As with all human potentials, how much he chooses to use this gift will depend on his self-image, on his level of motivation and on the opportunities he has had in life. If he was uninterested at school, he would have been the lazy type who could get by with the bare minimum of work and yet still manage to pass the necessary exams. As a motivated, hard working student, he would have been top or near-top of the class in all his chosen subjects. When someone with this type of brain is presented with new information relating to his work or interests, he seems almost instantly to understand and assimilate it without needing to reason or analyse. When someone's writing indicates that he is a quick thinker, you can be sure that he is highly intelligent. It is very likely that his IQ score will be in the top ten per cent of the population.

Signs to look for: handwriting **of any style** that satisfies one or more of these points:

1 The small letter 'g' shaped like a number 8 or an elogated letter 's'. The 'g' must be at the beginning of a word to be valid (check that you find 3 or more 'g's where this applies).

gone got gum give grill glad

2 The capital or small letter 'm' like 2 or 3 joined letter 'i's without dots (you need to see 3 or more 'm's made this way).

iiet name Mary home my Man

3 The small letter 'r' with two peaks; the first **must be** noticeably higher (look for 4 or more 'r's with this shape).

water rest early letters heart

4 A single crossbar used for 3 letter 't's in the same word, or for 2 which are **not** side by side (you need to find 2 or more places where this happens).

attention attractive statement

The Versatile Mind

This person has an unusual mind, indicating a balanced development of the right and left hemispheres of the brain. The left hemisphere is the part of the brain responsible for scientific and analytical thinking processes, utilising reason and logic. The right hemisphere is active when the brain is functioning creatively, using intuition and artistic perception. He is likely to have achieved a good academic balance in both the arts and the sciences at school.

His supple mind can easily attune itself to changing circumstances without losing composure. Thoughts flow smoothly and an adaptable social manner enables him to get on with a wide range of different personality types. This versatile intelligence will allow him to be successful in a wide range of careers. If he has the motivation, he could be an effective manager, as he would be able to handle the unpredictable and changing demands that frequently confront someone in such a position, changing tack to solve problems by approaching them from a different angle. His resourceful nature is always open to new ideas and ways of achieving objectives. The only real drawback to possessing a variety of talents is that if he chooses a line of employment utilising only a small area of his abilities, the remaining unexpressed potentials are likely to create in him a strong sense of unfulfilment. If he is to achieve a feeling of real accomplishment, he needs a job or some other means of self-expression which calls for a fusion of creative intuitive thought with logical and analytical reasoning.

Signs to look for: handwriting **of any style** that satisfies **three** or more of these points:

1 The small letter 'm' sharply angled at the bottom — it may also have sharp angles at the top (watch for 2 or more 'm's made this way).

met am man my dim Me Mat am

2 The capital or small letter 'm' like 2 or 3 joined letter 'i's without dots (you need to see 2 or more 'm's like this).

iiet naiiie Mary home my Man

3 The small letter 'r' with two peaks; the first **must be** noticeably higher (be sure you find 2 or more 'r's with this shape).

water rest early letters heart

4 The small letter 'm' with rounded, level tops (look for 2 or more 'm's like this).

many main am mix most my

5 The small letter 'g' shaped like a number 8 or an elongated letter 's'. The 'g' must be the first letter in a word to be vaild (check that you spot 2 or more).

gone got gum give grill glad

The Methodical Mind

Faced with a problem to solve, he needs time to process ideas and facts until every piece falls into place, and only then, after close consideration of all available information, will he draw conclusions. He will not grasp new ideas especially quickly either, but once he has learnt something you can be sure he will retain it well. His mind is not very well adapted to the study of theoretical subjects which have no practical application. These types are often wrongly classified as less intelligent than fast-thinking students. Where subjects do call for practical application, methodical thinkers are high achievers, especially suited to artistic professions requiring the skilful use of their hands, or to jobs in electronics or mechanics or certain areas of the building industry, where it can be necessary to pay methodical attention to detail and not make hasty decisions.

Signs to look for: handwriting **of any style** that satisfies either of these points:

1 Writing in which the small letter 'm' nearly always has rounded, level tops.

many main am MIX most my

2 Writing in which the small letter 'm' nearly always has flat, level tops.

game dream machine Mixing

The Analytical Mind

This person does not base his opinions on hearsay, but conducts his own fact-finding research and assesses the available information thoroughly before coming to a conclusion. He then rigidly sticks to his viewpoints, as he has invested much time in forming them and is usually stubbornly convinced that they are right. It should be clear that this individual is by no means gullible: when presented with new ideas or concepts, no matter how plausible they seem, he will meticulously evaluate their worth and be quick to point out any weaknesses or faults. Should problems crop up at work he will try hard to pinpoint their source and offer remedies, which he will readily be able to justify.

Signs to look for: handwriting **of any style** that satisfies this point:

1 The small letter 'm' sharply angled at the bottom (look for 4 or more 'm's like this). It may also have sharp angles at the top and if so, then also see 'The Inquisitive Type'.

met am man my dim Me mat am

GETTING RESULTS

The chapters in this section describe those aspects of human nature which will determine the strength of an individual's ability to survive and succeed. These basic traits relate equally to work situations and to personal relationships.

The Focused Mind

This person can concentrate his attention single-mindedly on one thing at a time. He never loses sight of his goals or gets out of touch with reality, for he has a mature and responsible attitude to life and always takes care of his obligations. In his work he is very conscientious and efficient and pays attention to detail. He is likely to have a very good memory for facts relating to his job. Because he has intellectual stamina, he will be able to work long hours and he will not be the type to complain about overtime. To sum up, he is likely to be a well disciplined, intelligent individual who will work hard to develop his potential and ambitions.

Signs to look for: handwriting **of any style** that satisfies one or more of these points:

1 The small letter 'i' with the dot **nearly always** very close to and directly above the stem.

if it is interesting it isnt difficult is it?

2 Handwriting composed entirely of precisely formed capital letters of uniform size, with evenly spaced words in straight lines.

LET IT BE AND TAKE IT EASY   BE HERE NOW !

3 Handwriting where the central zone is as small or smaller than this:

along : something : regarding : anything : surprising : thing : interesting → CENTRAL ZONE

The Self-confident Type

This person has a general underlying feeling that he will be successful in his endeavours. Even if he does not succeed, he will not take it personally and view himself as a failure but will simply try again or alternatively set his sights on another goal. He will be at least moderately successful in the line of work he chooses and his attitude to life will inspire those he deals with to have faith in him. In social situations he will communicate well and his manner will be self-assured.

Signs to look for: handwriting **of any style** that satisfies one or more of these points:

1 Any signature where the first name merges with the surname.

2 Any signature underlined by a single line detached from the signature.

3 Capital letters, in writing or signature, at least 3½ times the size of the central zone (you need to find 2 or more letters this size).

4 Handwriting where the central zone is as large or larger than this:

CENTRAL
ZONE

The Persistent Type

This person's temperament enables him to keep moving towards a goal in spite of obstacles and temporary setbacks. He is not easily discouraged and certainly never loses heart for long: when he sets his mind on something, he can take hard blows and even repeated defeats and yet still not give up until he succeeds. This inbuilt resilience to failure will be an obvious asset in his work: once he starts something, he will have the necessary psychological strength to see it through to completion rather than quit when the going gets tough. This quality will allow him to take the good with the bad in a close relationship – he will not easily 'abandon ship'.

Signs to look for: handwriting **of any style** that satisfies one or more of these points:

1 The capital letter 'A', 'H' or 'R' tied with a knot (check that you find 2 or more letters where this applies).

A A R R H H

2 The small letter 'f', 's' or 't' tied with a knot (make sure you have 2 or more letters like this).

for of fun the too but cat sit base

3 The capital or small letter 't' with a crossbar having a hook on the righthand side. There may also be a hook on the lefthand side as well (look for 2 or more 't's like this).

Tony Tom To at got cat put too it at

4 Any of the small letters with a final hook on the ending. The letter must be at the end of a word to be valid (you need to find 2 or more letters with this).

and are cat man though am all

5 Any of the small letters where the ending extends horizontally. The letter must be at the end of a word to be valid (look for 2 or more places where this happens).

bed see tough feel Sum gun mat

6 The small letter 't' where the crossbar forms a star-shape to the left of the stem (watch for 2 or more 't's with this shape).

nut hat get pet

Initiative

This person possesses far more than his fair share of natural common sense. He is endowed with an inborn sense of responsibility motivating him to prompt action and does not require supervision when a job needs doing – he is more than capable of generating his own momentum and will be able to see what needs to be done without being told. At work, his keen eye locates any opportunity to streamline actions by cutting out unnecessary details, thereby allowing him to remain alert and on the ball, even in stressful environments. He will undoubtedly be conscientious, efficient and resourceful and because he is flexible, can shift direction as the situation warrants. You can rely on him to be practical-minded and realistic in his approach and, when necessary, to make quick, sensible decisions.

Signs to look for: handwriting **of any style** that satisfies one or more of these points:

1 Any ascending signature underlined by a single ascending line.

Jim Jones   *Mary Brown*   *Don Burrows*

2 A single crossbar used for 3 letter 't's in the same word, or for 2 which are **not** side by side (make sure you find 2 or more places where this happens).

attention   *attractive*   *statement*

3 The small letter 't' where the crossbar is formed by an ascending line to the right of the stem without lifting the pen from the paper. The 't' must be at the end of a word to be valid (watch for 2 or more words where this applies).

that   what   quit   first   Knot   great

4 The small letter 'g' or 'y' with a line ascending to the right resembling the letter 'q' you need to find 2 or more letters like this).

gone   fig   age   giving   you   buy   rye

The Determined Type

This person is endowed with a deep-rooted, strong determination very physical in its origin, for it is not the product of either the intellect or the personality but stems from an innate physical drive that lies within the biological survival mechanism. Because this type of determination is based mainly on physical energy, it is weakened by ill-health to a far greater degree than related traits such as persistence and assertiveness, which are offshoots of the intellect and personality.

An individual with this sort of determination will devote himself wholeheartedly to any job he undertakes until he has seen it through to completion. He is certainly not a quitter and can be relied upon to work long hours, for he has well above average stamina and a strong survival instinct, and will be prepared to fight his way out of troubled times. This driving force will overcome most obstacles and even if other related success traits are not present in his personality, he will invariably succeed in achieving his ambitions because this particular quality of determination is sufficiently powerful even on its own.

Signs to look for: handwriting **of any style** that satisfies one or more of these points:

1 The small letter 'd', 'h', 'm', 'n' or 't' with an ending that descends noticeably below the base of the letter (you must see 2 or more letters like this).

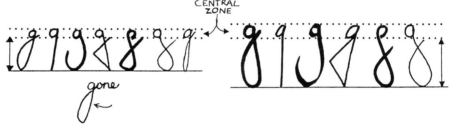

2 The small letter 'g' with a descending line at least 3½ times the size of the central zone (you need to see 3 or more 'g's where this happens).

3 The small letter 'g' or 'y' with a very firm and straight descending line (look for 3 or more letters like this).

The Forward Planner

When this individual has a job to do he likes to assess available facts carefully and then form a clear plan of procedure. He generally avoids handling situations spontaneously as he likes to draw on past experiences in order to pre-plan, and before carrying out a task is likely already to have visualised its completion. He feels very uneasy if he is unable to finish what he is doing, for he detests leaving loose ends that will be in constant conflict with the 'finished' visualised picture in his head. His motivation to conclude whatever he begins comes both from his incapacity to tolerate unfinished business and from the fact that he is by nature a person who is goal-oriented and ambitious, with a sense of responsibility, someone who will take care of his obligations.

Signs to look for: handwriting **of any style** that satisfies one or more of these points:

1 Writing in which almost every word has its letters fully joined together.

everything changing letting the past go by

2 Writing with very straight lines maintained throughout where heavy pen pressure makes indentations that show clearly on the reverse of the paper.

goals clearly set   Just make a decision

3 The small letter 'g' or 'y' with an ascending line that nearly always reaches the central zone or higher.

g g g g y y y y   ← CENTRAL ZONE

4 The small letter 't' where the crossbar is just fractionally below the top of the stem and nearly as long or even longer than the stem (make sure you see 3 or more 't's where this applies).

best it hat met art eat

5 A single crossbar used for 3 letter 't's in the same word, or for 2 which are **not** side by side (look for 2 or more words where this happens).

attention attractive statement

The Assertive Type

This person has a very strong will. His approach to life is enthusiastic and energised, he has a sense of purpose and therefore seems to have a clearer idea than most about what can be expected from life. He has no problems in making decisions, his goals are self-made and he needs no direction from others with regard to his career, for he is extremely self-motivated and will strive hard to work either independently or in a position where he has authority over others. Indeed, he is unlikely to tolerate those who have authority over him, having a fundamentally competitive, ambitious nature and a demanding ego – he needs to achieve a significant amount of success in life in order to feel good about himself. He has an excellent chance of being very successful in his chosen career, and a good provider.

When he decides to do something, it will be very difficult to dissuade him for he is both persistent and determined to succeed at any cost. A partner may well find him too assertive and headstrong at times: he can be unnecessarily rigid in his views and will invariably try to get his own way. He is bound to make more than his fair share of decisions and needs to be careful not to become bossy, domineering and self-righteous.

Signs to look for: handwriting **of any style** that satisfies one or more of these points:

1 Capital or small letter 't' with a crossbar at least twice as long as the stem (watch for 4 or more 't's like this).

Tea Tom too tip it

2 The small letter 't' with a crossbar that **noticeably** thickens on one side (you will need to find 2 or more 't's where this happens).

cat at get it hot nut

3 The small letter 'g' or 'y' with a sharply angled triangle **of any shape** (watch for 2 or more triangles like this).

4 The small letter 'h', 'm' **and** 'n' sharply angled at the top and bottom (be sure you spot 4 or more **of each** letter).

mahogany HUMAN handsome

Exceptional Endurance

This person has a strong instinct for survival. His ambition for material security is unusually high and he is not frightened by hard work, so he is bound to be devoted to his job and will be a tireless worker who requires little rest or diversion. His physical stamina and ambitious nature provide him with more than enough impetus to see things through to their finish, but as his determination stems largely from a genetically physical nature it is susceptible to being weakened by illness, unlike the more intellect-based traits of persistence and assertiveness.

He is practical-minded and realistic so he does not expect any free rides in life, being likely to emerge a winner through his own hard efforts. He enjoys challenges but achievement gives him only temporary satisfaction, and then his mind becomes quickly absorbed in his next project. When he has nothing to do he becomes extremely frustrated, for he cannot stand monotony and likes to be constantly on the move and productive. His fighting spirit thrives on competition, since he is motivated by a continual need to prove to himself, as well as others, that he is a successful human being.

He can be somewhat difficult as a partner because he always wants to be doing things and finds it almost impossible to sit still, relax and take it easy without quickly becoming restless. With such high levels of physical energy, a daily session of physical exercise is a necessity so that he can gain more enjoyment from his leisure time, and be a more easy-going partner. He will, however, be a very successful provider, able to hold his ground when times get rough.

Signs to look for: handwriting **of any style** that satisfies either or both of these points:

1 The small letter 'g' with a descending line at least 3½ times the size of the central zone (ensure that you identify 3 or more 'g's where this happens).

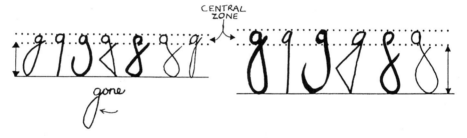

CENTRAL ZONE

gone

2 Writing where heavy pen pressure makes indentations that clearly show on the reverse of the paper.

DOMINANT CHARACTERISTICS

Signs in the writing of any of the following characteristics will reveal aspects of personality deeply rooted in a person's innermost nature that strongly influence his behaviour and outlook on life.

If you should uncover a trait that does not seem to fit someone's outward manner, remember that only those exceptionally close to them will be aware of it. Also, characteristics appearing in the same writing occasionally interact either to increase or reduce one another's influence on actual behaviour. For example, 'The Chatterbox' will become almost unbearably talkative if he also has the trait of 'The Restless Dreamer', for he will have an unlimited number of ideas to express from his vivid and over-active imagination. On the other hand, 'The Over-sensitive' will be less tiresome and touchy if they also have the trait of 'The Humourous Type'. Indeed, it will be obvious to most readers that characteristics such as humour, sympathy and optimism will inevitably 'lighten' the somewhat negative effect on behaviour produced by traits such as impatience, hysteria and, clearly, physical aggression.

The Master Diplomat

This person can assess someone's personality and state of mind and adapt his own behaviour to create a harmonious atmosphere. He is very tactful and will never offend or upset others. When people argue he will try to smooth things over, or withdraw to avoid worsening matters. He will definitely not make social blunders, neither is it in his nature to cast blame on others. If someone makes a mistake he will do his best to render it insignificant or, if possible, act as if he had not noticed. His capacity to avoid emotional conflicts will ensure that even if his partner is argumentative or over-sensitive, their relationship stays relatively peaceful.

Signs to look for: handwriting **of any style** that satisfies either or both of these points:

1 The capital or small letter 'm' with 3 parts that **gradually diminish** in height without losing legibility. A sudden drop in height in the letter is not valid (make sure you see 2 or more 'm's that diminish in height gradually).

Monaco Mandy time Lime

2 Any word (with 3 or more letters) in which the letters **gradually diminish** in height from the beginning to the end of the word (look for 2 or more words where this happens).

Swim Car Mean game pan

The Sympathetic Type

This individual can sense the thoughts and feelings of others with uncanny accuracy, a most valuable gift. When people talk to him they will sense that he is listening sympathetically, with full attention and interest. He really knows how to make others feel he is totally on their wavelength and can establish a rapport remarkably quickly. He is naturally sensitive and responsive to the differing needs of those he deals with – he can communicate effectively with a wide range of personality types and will have a convincing and persuasive way of expressing himself, because he is able to touch not only the intellects but also the hearts of those he meets. He could be very successful in public relations or in any job requiring well developed social skills. In a managerial position, his warm understanding nature will allow him to cope smoothly with the needs and personal problems of employees.

In a close relationship he has the potential to be exceptionally sensitive, good-natured and understanding, considerate enough to know when something is bothering his partner and able to respond to her needs. He will be very devoted to those he really cares about, going out of his way to help his friends and unlikely ever to turn his back on someone in trouble. However, if someone criticises him or gives out any form of negative vibration he will be easily hurt, for his sensitivity has made him very vulnerable to attack and he is affected far more than most by an unfriendly or condemnatory atmosphere.

Signs to look for: handwriting **of any style** that satisfies points 1 or 2 **and** one or more of the other points:

1 The small letter 'd' or 't' with a looped stem (you need to spot 4 or more stems this size).

and road bed dog doing too at mat eat

2 The small letter 'g' or 'y' with a line ascending to the right resembling the letter 'q' except that the base must be **rounded** (look for 2 or more letters with this sign).

give right dog might yes year day eyes

3 The small letter 'd', 'e', 'h', 'm', 'n' or 't' with a cup-shaped ending. The letter must be at the end of a word to be valid (make sure you find 4 or more letters that end this way).

and hid though am can are nut at

4 The small letters 'a' **and** 'o' that are nearly always very rounded and also **clear** inside.

good food as always can you come again soon?

5 The small letter 'i' with the dot nearly always small and round.

This investigation is limiting his rights!

6 Writing that leans, even slightly, to the right (writing that leans to the right more than the following example is **not** valid).

Understanding feelings is the key

The Over-sensitive Type

This person has an ego which is easily bruised. He cares far too much about the opinions others have of him and is always on guard against direct or subtle verbal attacks. He will register a put-down no matter how indirect or unobtrusive it may be, and his extra-clear memory of emotional hurts will not allow him to forget.

Living with such an individual is by no means easy: because he is hypersensitive, he may at times misinterpret even well-meant advice as personal criticism, and will react by becoming very upset and angry. The roots of this behavioural pattern inevitably trace back to a childhood in which he experienced frequent disapproval from others, either in the family or at school. He seems to be suffering from the after-effects of an overdose of criticism which has made him perpetually afraid of being hurt. These childhood experiences have made him emotionally very insecure; though he may not be aware of it, he has an intense fear of rejection. This has made it very difficult for him to feel that others accept him and that is why he over-reacts when he thinks he is being criticised. Consequently, in an intimate relationship he becomes deeply upset if his partner criticises him because he subconsciously fears that this could mean she doesn't really love him. The positive side of the situation is that he has a sentimental nature and is capable of being a sympathetic partner if treated the right way. He will be encouraged by compliments to a far greater degree than the average person, and you can be sure of winning his affection if you feed him with the good vibrations he badly needs to strengthen his vulnerable ego.

Letter 'd's which have extra wide, balloon-shaped stems, as in point 2, indicate someone suffering from a greatly exaggerated fear that others strongly disapprove of his personality and conduct. All the aspects of behaviour mentioned previously, associated with over-reacting to criticism, will be exaggerated to the extreme in his personality. He will frequently believe that others are criticising him when clearly they are not; even if they are silent, he assumes that they are critical of him in their thoughts. He is quite definitely a manifestation of the persecution complex.

Signs to look for: handwriting **of any style** that satisfies either of these points:

1 The small letter 'd' with a looped stem which is at least as wide as the central zone (check you see 2 or more 'd's like this).

2 The small letter 'd' with a looped stem which is at least twice as wide as the central zone (you must find 2 or more 'd's where this applies).

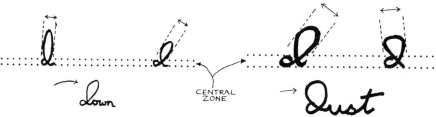

The Liar

This person might have thoroughly good intentions towards other people and merely tell them harmless tall stories or white lies. In exaggerated form, this kind of behaviour may reveal itself in his choice of job – salesman or advertising executive, gossip columnist or politician – professions which inevitably require a significant 'stretching of the truth'. It is possible, however, that lies form an essential part of his daily survival kit, and that he will not hesitate to evade, disguise, distort or smother the truth in order to achieve his aims – usually at other people's expense, though if he is found out, of course, it could be to his own cost. In business, he may mislead and manipulate others, or hide his real intentions, till a deal is clinched. In love, he may disguise the truth about his sex life. And, most significant of all, he will not feel guilty about it, but believe himself to be fully justified in his behaviour and compelled to continue in it.

Points 1 and 2 are not valid for the writing of people with dyslexia or other spelling difficulties.

Signs to look for: handwriting **of any style** that satisfies one or more of these points:

1 Legible writing with words missing a whole letter (you need to find 3 or more words where this happens). This rule does not apply to letters that are missing due to excessive speed of writing.

difficult thinking accident

2 Legible writing with words missing part of a letter so as to alter the identity of that letter. This rule does not apply to the small letters 'e', 'r' or 't' or to parts of letters that are missing due to excessive speed of writing.

exciting adventure   *uaterfall renember?*

missing portion changes 'd' to 'l'   missing portion changes 'w' to 'u'   missing portion changes 'm' to 'n'

3 The small letter 'a', 'c', 'o' or 'g' made with a double or treble loop (check that there are 3 more letters that have this sign).

remain advance precisely look flag

The Optimist

This individual has chosen to look at the bright side of life – he seems to have an inner faith that everything will turn out fine in the end and his positive mental attitude will not let him brood over circumstances he cannot alter. Even in the face of misfortune he will quickly recover from any feelings of disappointment and will usually manage to see something of value in the situation. He is likely to be fairly ambitious, with drive, determination and self-assurance. He can become extremely absorbed and possessed by any projects which stimulate his interest, and will feel confident of achieving his goals.

His optimistic nature generates enthusiasm and energy, and endows him with high spirits and a cheerful countenance. He is likely to make friends easily, for his good-humoured, expressive manner will be very appealing. He enjoys talking to people and his positive *joie de vivre* can be quite infectious. His partner is likely to benefit from his sunny, optimistic ways: if she has a tendency to become depressed or pessimistic, he may well be able to draw her out of such moods with his passion for living and positive outlook.

Signs to look for: handwriting **of any style** that satisfies one or more of these points:

1 Any ascending signature.

Saul Wallis   Vic Cole   Cleo Ryman   Geoffrey

2 Any ascending line of writing (you need to see 3 or more lines where this happens).

try to get in touch with your feelings
your attitude influences you whole life!

3 The capital or small letter 't' with the crossbar sloping upwards (look for 3 or more 't's with this).

Time   To   This   but   at   too

4 The capital or small letter 't' with the crossbar at least 3 times as long as the stem (you must find 4 or more 't's where this applies).

Them   Tune   get   to

5 The small letter 'd', 'e', 'h', 'm', 'n' or 't' with an ending that rises noticeably high. The letter must be at the end of a word to be valid (make sure you spot 4 or more words with this ending).

and   are   though   gum   fun   yet

The Chatterbox

This person dissipates his energy with incessant talking. You will never have to push him to give you his opinions because he will voice them willingly, whether you like it or not. Being a compulsive talker, he will feel uncomfortable in moments of silence if he is with someone he does not know well, and will immediately try to plug the gaps with chatter. His telephone bills are likely to be astronomic. Sigmund Freud would probably have classified him as orally fixated. Indeed, it is quite probable that when not engaged in conversation he will fill his oral cavity with a cigar, a cigarette, chewing gum or maybe just his fingernails. Alternatively, he could well be a compulsive nibbler who eats frequently between meals and then complains he has trouble keeping his weight down.

His non-stop conversation allows him to conceal his emotions, both from himself and from others: he finds this area of life difficult to handle. The problem with this tactic is that it has unwanted side-effects: by talking too much, he is unable to reach a deep level of connection with those around him, since he forces communication to remain at the superficial level of the intellect. In other words, his manner of communication is a barrier which keeps others at arm's length, blocking the opportunity for expressing and receiving the heartfelt feelings that occur at deeper levels of human interaction.

He also tends to brood over conflicts he has had with others, with the result that he constantly re-stimulates the negative emotion he felt during the actual situation – he is continually stoking the fire of his own angry feelings. Because of this, he loses perspective and exaggerates the importance of what may have been merely trivial disagreements. It can take a great deal of time for him to re-establish feelings of harmony within himself if he feels he has been wronged. He needs to learn to allow his partner time to speak, as he can monopolise conversation. He is also a poor listener, because he is usually too busy thinking about his reply to tune accurately into what is being said. Compulsive talkers are often extremely physical human beings, with an abundance of stamina. A good portion of their chattering is their body's way of releasing unused physical energy that would be better expressed through sport or some other physical activity.

Signs to look for: handwriting **of any style** that satisfies this point:

1 The small letters 'a' **and** 'o' with a wide gap at the top (you must find 4 or more **of each** letter).

To go away one day always good food

one makes too many arrangements

The Absentminded Type

This person is the type who has great difficulty in remembering just where he has put his car keys or, if he wears glasses, he will probably spend more time looking for them than he does actually wearing them. His partner would do well to remember exactly where he parks his car when they go out together or else they could spend more time searching for it afterwards than they do on their shopping or entertainment. Also, she should be aware that he may forget birthdays and anniversaries, not because he does not care, but because he cannot seem to help it.

There are two possible underlying causes for this syndrome. He may be one of those individuals with such a busy life that he has a thousand and one important items on his mind and consequently becomes so lost in his thoughts that when performing an action as mundane as putting his keys down, his hand and body are in one place but his mind is elsewhere. Alternatively, he might be the lackadaisical, lazy sort who spends his time day-dreaming and does not pay adequate attention to what he is doing.

Though the personalities behind these two examples may be poles apart, the root underlying cause of absentmindedness is the same. In both situations, the individuals are suffering from a mind/body disconnection, or split, and to cure this problem they need to make a conscious effort to unify mind with body while performing any action. Absentmindedness is a universal characteristic, for we all, at times, are doing things with our body – for example, eating – while our thoughts are miles away: in other words, our mind is literally absent from our body. Most of us, however, have developed the habit of remaining mentally present during the performance of such actions as putting down car keys because the aggravation caused by lost keys is considered unbearable. Those who are labelled absentminded simply have not yet disciplined themselves in this area.

Signs to look for: handwriting **of any style** that satisfies one or more of these points:

1 Writing in which at least half the small letter 'i's are without dots.

If this is irritating it is a pity it didn't fit

2 The small letter 't' that has neither a crossbar **nor any variation** of one (look for 2 or more 't's like this).

what is that question time goes too fast

3 The small letter 't' with the crossbar floating above the stem (you need to see 4 or more 't's like this).

that is not right what is this to you?

The Showman

This person is able to present convincingly any image of himself that he chooses, adapting his manner, clothing and conversation in order to show himself in the best possible light. A businessman with this trait will wear a smart, tastefully chosen suit and really look the part; a laid-back type will have a suitably 'cool' appearance. His behaviour is intended to impress others, as he has a strong inner desire to be admired and respected; he will know just how to seem very well informed and reliable even if this is not the case. He has excellent social presence and should do very well in interviews: when he wishes to get his ideas across, he can be very persuasive. He inspires others to have confidence in him, for even if he does not have faith in himself he will speak and move with assurance, and he is able easily to switch on charisma and friendliness while still being responsive to those with whom he communicates. Showmanship is quite obviously an ideal, even necessary trait in selling, politics, acting and any other career calling for good communication.

If you are beginning a relationship with this person, make sure you probe deeply beneath the surface of his apparent personality for you may discover you are with a completely different human being.

Signs to look for: handwriting **of any style** that satisfies one or more of these points:

1 Any signature that is quite obviously large or showy.

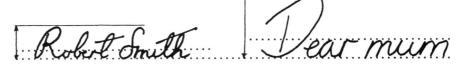

2 Capital letters in writing or signature at least 3½ times the size of the central zone (make sure you see 2 or more capitals where this applies).

3 Lower stems with an over-inflated balloon appearance of any shape (make sure you spot 4 or more stems like this).

4 Looped upper stems with an over-inflated balloon appearance of any shape (you need to find 4 or more stems like this). The letters 'd' and 't' cannot be used as examples.

The Restless Dreamer

This person has an over-active imagination making it hard for him to concentrate, as he has to struggle to avoid being sidetracked by stimulating but unrelated ideas. He needs to develop a more realistic attitude to life. The vivid world of his imagination will also make him physically and mentally restless. He could well suffer from insomnia. Possessed by a thousand unfulfilled desires, he finds reality desperately dull. In a close relationship he will never find contentment. The person to satisfy his needs does not exist on Planet Earth. When space travel is thriving, he will be the type to rocket in search of the perfect cosmic mate. He finds freedom from the grip of his frustrated feelings only through his limitless sexual fantasy, where he can play his ideal role of super-rich, super-powerful super-lover.

Signs to look for: handwriting **of any style** that satisfies **both** these points:

1 Looped upper stems with an over-inflated balloon appearance of any shape (you need to find 4 or more stems like this). The letters 'd' and 't' cannot be used as examples.

2 The small letter 'g' with an over-inflated balloon appearance **of any shape** (make sure you find 3 or more 'g's that look like this).

The Pennypincher

This person will be unusually possessive of his personal belongings and will enjoy gloating over any valuables he has accumulated. He is bound to be tight-fisted; in a pub, where everyone is taking their turn to buy a round, he will time things perfectly so that the bell signalling closing time rings just before his turn to place an order. He feels like a businessman who has just pulled off a good deal when he comes away from a social gathering having received more than he has given – as long as he can get away with this unnoticed. His partner will have to work very hard to persuade him to lay out money for anything he considers to be an unnecessary luxury item, but on the positive side, he is likely to be skilful at making an economically secure life for them both.

Signs to look for: handwriting **of any style** that satisfies either or both of these points:

1 The small letter 'y' with a stem that curls under like an eagle's talon (watch for 2 or more 'y's with this appearance).

2 The capital letter 'E' with spiral formations top and bottom (you must see 2 or more 'E's like this).

The Loyal Type

This person is extremely ethical in his attitude to friendship and its obligations. He is likely to be socially very selective, limiting himself to a few close companions, since he prefers to avoid superficial encounters. Those whom he chooses as friends will find him reliable and faithful to his commitments – when he makes a promise it will be of utmost importance to him that he keeps it. He is the sort who would stand by his friends and physically fight to defend them even if he knew his fighting skills were useless, for he would never turn his back on someone in trouble.

Because of the high value he places on friendship, he will naturally be bitterly disappointed if he is let down by broken promises, for the trust and companionship he gives to others are what he expects in return. He is very likely to be a faithful partner, who can be relied upon in times of need, and who will stay permanently with the one he seriously chooses to be with. The only exceptions to this would be if he felt betrayed by his loved one in any way, or if he was possessed by uncontrollable sexual energy, which can potentially undermine the values of even the most ethical human being.

Signs to look for: handwriting **of any style** that satisfies **all** these points:

1 Writing in which at least half the small letter 'i's have a dot that is both small and round.

This investigation is limiting his rights

2 Writing in which the small letters 'a' **and** 'o' are nearly always **clear** inside.

soon you can come again looking good again

3 Writing with **a complete absence** of the graphological signs described in 'The Liar'.

The Stubborn Mule

This person has an essentially dogmatic nature. His rigid, inflexible attitudes narrow his perspective and cause him to be unreasonably obstinate at times. He is very unreceptive to other people's ideas when they conflict with his own and will vehemently argue to defend his point of view, disinclined to change his mind even in the face of logic and reason, for he feels that to do so would an act of weakness.

In his work there will be friction between himself and any superiors who treat him as anything less than an equal. He strongly resents being given orders as he has a very rebellious nature and dislikes authority, resisting whenever possible any attempts by others to dominate him. He is not someone who simply falls obediently in line and blindly follows orders, in fact he will blatantly refuse to do what he is told if he feels he is right or if the order is given disrespectfully, for he is the type who openly stands up for what he believes in. On the positive side, when faced with a difficult problem he will not give up until he has found a solution, because his obstinate personality will not allow him to accept defeat.

He will need to learn the meaning of the word compromise if he wishes to avoid much unnecessary unhappiness at home. His difficult nature can make him a stressful person to live with unless his partner is extremely passive and content to give in to his way of doing and thinking.

Signs to look for: handwriting **of any style** that satisfies one or more of these points:

1 The small letter 'd' or 't' with a stem that forms a tent-shape (you need to find 3 or more shapes like this).

dog and pad idea at it but hit

2 The small letter 'd' or 't' with an ending that descends noticeably below the base of the letter (check you find 3 or more letters that do this).

and bed rod lid fit hit pet

3 The small letter 't' where the crossbar forms a star-shape to the left of the stem (watch for 3 or more 't's with this shape).

nut hat get pet

4 The capital or small letter 'm' with 2 sharp, **upright** peaks of equal height (you must see 3 or more 'm's where this applies).

Mandy sum pram am my

5 The small letter 'g' or 'y' with a sharply angled triangle **of any shape** (watch for 2 or more triangles like this).

6 The small letters 'h', 'm' **and** 'n' sharply angled at the top and bottom (you will need to spot 4 or more **of each** letter).

mahogany human handsome

The Culture Lover

Strongly moved by fine examples of artistic work, this person has the soul of a connoisseur and a natural affinity with beauty. He will probably have a yearning to express himself creatively and if he finds no suitable outlet will sublimate this desire through immense enjoyment of the artistic endeavours of others. Aesthetically agreeable surroundings will usually be a necessity if he is to feel at ease. He could well be the sort who loves sweet-smelling soap for his bath and all sorts of delicate trimmings that stimulates his fine senses. More than most, he will appreciate luxury and ease and, given the chance, will gravitate towards the finer things in life. This person will have a well above average sensitivity for matters of culture, such as theatre, jazz or classical music, opera, architecture, archaeology or some other field of artistic expression.

Signs to look for: handwriting **of any style** that satisfies **two** or more of these points:

1 Writing done from choice with a medium or thick felt-tip pen, or any other pen producing broad thick lines.

Relaxation **feelings** **Awareness**

2 Handwriting neatly framed by wide, even margins on all four sides.

3 The small letter 'd' where the stem is a single ascending line curving to the left (look for 3 or more 'd's where this happens).

dog grade day dim lic mud

4 The capital or small letter 'e' shaped like a backward-facing number 3 (you must spot 3 or more 'e's like this).

Edna egg meal Easy pet End

5 The small letter 'f' shaped like a treble clef (you need to find 3 or more 'f's like this).

felicity fat f far drift for

6 The small letter 'g' shaped like a number 8 or an elongated letter 's'. The 'g' must be at the beginning of a word to be valid (look for 3 or more of these 'g's).

gone got gum give grill glad

The Physically Aggressive

The graphological signs of physical aggression described here are the only ones I have come across which stand on their own as reliable indicators of this trait. If they do not appear, physically aggressive tendencies could still be present in the personality but would then have to be deduced by analysis of many different handwriting features which could not be explained in a book such as this. If the writing reveals any of the first five points you are dealing with someone who has an aggressive will and who feels a strong compulsion to control people. He will be quick to retaliate if he encounters any form of aggression from others and when emotionally aroused can turn into a one-man stampede. If all else fails, and he feels he is losing ground in a confrontation, he could erupt and settle the argument with his fists. Writing that reveals point 6 indicates someone who possesses enormous physical energy. Unfortunately, emotional blockages in the form of subconsciously repressed hostile feelings, are hindering its free expression and causing it to build up. Unless he has an extremely physical job which releases of some of this pressure, he could well express his pent-up energy destructively in a violent, cruel and even sadistic fashion, though this side of his nature will be hidden from all but the unfortunate few.

Please note: a female with handwriting indicating physical aggression is likely to exhibit violent behaviour less frequently than a male with the same characteristic. This is largely due to Western cultural conditioning, which makes it far less acceptable for females to express anger physically. However, there is also evidence that this difference may be partly influenced by the presence of testosterone in men. This male hormone has, as a result of work carried out by scientists, been linked with raised levels of physical aggression.

Signs to look for: handwriting **of any style** that satisfies points 1 **and** 2, **or** one or more of the other points:

1 The small letters 'h', 'm' **and** 'n' nearly always sharply angled at the top and bottom and written in such a **heavy-handed** manner that their indentations show clearly on the reverse of the paper.

mahogany *HUMAN* *handsome*

2 Any letters clogged with ink (you must find 4 or more letters where this can be seen).

what is that *Come back* *look at it*

3 The small letter 't' with the crossbar sloping downwards and **noticeably** thicker at the end (make certain you identify 3 or more 't's like this).

hit *hot* *fat* *it* *but*

4 The small letter 'd' or 't' with an ending that thickens as it descends noticeably below the base of the letter (be sure you find 3 or more letters that do this).

red *bed* *hid* *nod* *at* *sit* *mat* *it* *cat*

5 The small letter 'd', 'e' or 't' with an extended horizontal or ascending ending that becomes **noticeably** thicker. The letter must be at the end of a word to be valid (you need to see 3 or more letters where this happens).

and *hid* *bit* *at* *are* *here*

6 The small letter 'g' or 'y' with a very firm and straight descending line that becomes **noticeably** thicker at the end (look for 4 or more letters that have this sign).

got *bag* *dig* *hug* *you* *try* *buy* *very*

The Human Squirrel

This person is a natural survivor with considerable strength of spirit, the type who never gives up. These qualities are probably the product of a childhood in which he experienced either a great deal of emotional suffering or material deprivation. Deep-rooted feelings of insecurity, which he may not even be aware of, have developed the squirrel complex in him: acquiring things in order to satisfy unfulfilled childhood needs. He could well be a model railway fanatic or a collector of stamps and coins. Alternatively, souvenirs or hoards of sentimental junk may be found tucked away in his room or the attic – not needed, used or looked at, just comfortingly there. Often such people, even if they have material wealth, can exhibit behavioural patterns more appropriate to conditions of shortage. The partner of a human squirrel might have to arrange periodic clear-outs in order to empty the home of rubbish – but needs to make sure he is sent to visit friends or relatives first, or else there could be an all-out fight.

Signs to look for: handwriting **of any style** that satisfies either or both of these points:

1 The capital letter 'E' with spiral formations at top and bottom (look for 2 or more 'E's that have this).

2 Capital or small letters with a hook or hooks (you need to find **at least** 4 letters with this).

The Impatient Type

This individual is quick to anger but may have learnt to hide it, though he will still experience the emotion inwardly just as strongly. If lacking in self-control he will immediately retaliate or become short-tempered if he encounters any form of aggression or delay. He is continually impatient because whatever he is doing his mind is several steps ahead – he is always aware of and worried about the things he has to take care of in the future. He is probably obsessed with productivity and efficiency and takes on more than he can comfortably handle. He needs to learn to slow down and relax more in the present. In social situations he will steer well clear of superficial conversation and will find long-winded or verbose talkers intensely irritating. He must learn to give more of himself and his time, and not rush his partner; and she, to avoid much unnecessary tension, should always try to make sure that he is not kept waiting.

Signs to look for: handwriting **of any style** that satisfies this point:

1 The small letter 't' with the crossbar on the right, detached from the stem (look for 3 or more 't's where this happens).

at too get hot but hit it

The Humorous Type

This person possesses a potentially lively sense of humour that allows him at times to see the absurdity of existence and even the comic nature of his own problems. This helps him to maintain a healthy perspective on life, for he avoids taking himself too seriously and can adapt to changing circumstances. His sense of humour goes hand in hand with intellectual flexibility as well as fine intuition and instinct; invariably, he will have an agile and penetrating mind. He has the gift of being able to crack a joke to lighten the atmosphere; sometimes his conversation will positively sparkle with refreshing spontaneity and even when stressed he does not seem to lose that twinkle in his eye. His ability to see the ridiculous side of things will be a valuable tool in helping him patch up any differences with his partner.

Signs to look for: handwriting **of any style** that satisfies one or more of these points:

1 Any signature with a wavy line underlining it.

2 Any signature underlined by a 'smile' line.

3 The small letter 'g' shaped like a number 8. The 'g' must be the first letter in a word to be valid (watch for 4 or more 'g's like this).

4 Capital or small letters incorporating a wavy line or using one to connect to another letter (you need to find 2 or more letters that do this).

5 Capital or small letters incorporating a 'smile' line (look for 2 or more letters that have this).

6 The small letter 'b', 'd', 'f', 'h' or 'l' with a looped stem **close** to the central zone (make sure you spot 3 or more letters with this).

CENTRAL
ZONE

The Hysterical Type

This person has a highly neurotic and over-emotional nature and when under pressure can become stressed to the point where he completely loses balance. His efforts to restrain himself have produced behaviour that oscillates between extreme over-control and, at the other end of the spectrum, hysterical outbursts. He can appear completely calm at one moment and then, in the next instant, explode in anger. Because he has such an emotional nature, one cannot rely on his assessments – at times he is very subjective and his judgement becomes clouded.

The root source of this behavioural problem is his hyper-sensitive nature, which makes him very vulnerable to negative emotional atmospheres. He simply cannot tolerate any form of hostile behaviour from others and is obviously totally unsuited to employment which requires him to deal with very pressured situations. If someone offends him they will certainly regret it! In the home environment, regular shouting matches and full-blown arguments will be inevitable unless his partner possesses exceptional self-control. But, on the positive side, his highly volatile temperament goes hand in hand with an essentially romantic, passionate nature. If treated well, he can be an extremely loving and faithful partner – but double-cross such an individual and you will have to bear the unpleasant consequences.

Signs to look for: handwriting **of any style** that satisfies either or both of these points:

1 The small letter 'd' that leans to the right **noticeably** more than the rest of the writing (you must see 2 or more 'd's that do this).

intended   collected   instructed   found

2 Writing with most of its letters joined together that leans so far to the right it looks as if it might fall over. Writing composed of capital letters is not valid.

emotions having unbearable intensity
trying to control almost uncontrollable impulses

The Gourmet

This individual has a very sensual nature and exceptionally sensitive tastebuds. Delicious food triggers off an abundance of digestive salivas and his active sense of taste allows him the most exquisitely pleasurable sensations which may even send shivers down his spine. This response indicates that he is experiencing a massive endorphin rush. Endorphins, or natural opiates, produce the feeling of

elation that is generated by enjoyable activities and also by sports. The gourmet, for some reason, is provided with a far greater quantity of these than the average man, and after a really fine culinary experience he is able to sit back and float in the oceanic sensations of this natural 'high' provided by Mother Nature. The drawback of such a capacity to enjoy food is that he becomes extraordinarily disappointed by a poor quality meal, as his refined sense of taste greatly magnifies any unpleasant flavours. He will therefore be an extremely fussy eater who would sometimes choose to eat nothing at all in preference to subjecting his palate to the torture of second-rate cooking. Someone whose handwriting includes the graphological sign described in point 3, denoting a strong force of natural animal instinct, could be inclined to lash out when angered.

The following description applies only to males with this handwriting trait: that old cliché which says 'the way to a man's heart is through his stomach' would certainly apply in his case. Indeed, he will be bitterly disappointed if his partner cannot provide him with suitable cuisine. Alternatively, if he has the finance to allow it, he will frequent fine restaurants rather than eat at home.

Signs to look for: handwriting **of any style** that satisfies one or more of these points:

1 Writing done from choice with a medium or thick felt-tip pen, or any other pen producing broad thick lines.

2 The small letter 'g' with an over-inflated balloon appearance **of any shape** (check you find 3 or more 'g's like this).

3 Any letters clogged with ink (you must see 3 or more letters where this applies).

The Pessimist

When lines and/or words droop and slope downwards, this may simply be a sign of physical fatigue – a tired hand and arm naturally sink slowly towards the writer's body and this causes the line of writing to slope downwards. Alternatively, it could be an indication of a temporary, passing state of mind – the writer may have been upset by some specific event which has caused him to feel a little bit down. Usually, however, these graphological signs reveal that the writer has a generally depressed and pessimistic outlook on life. Sad feelings dominate his consciousness. He feels beaten, helpless and discouraged, anxious and self-questioning, and doubts that life will improve. This condition robs him of energy, weakens his spirit and considerably reduces his enthusiasm for everything, so that his efficiency will be impaired and he will have to compensate for this by increasing his self-discipline to over-ride his lowered vitality.

He has an extremely narrow and restricted perception of reality: he only sees the negative and darker aspects of existence, and because he is blind to the more positive side of life often feels that living is futile. This attitude may have been triggered originally by job-related failures and/or bad domestic trouble. If this is so and if both these areas of life improve enough, the depression may disperse. If not, this individual should seek either the help of close friends prepared to listen to his troubles, or enter some form of respected psychotherapy.

Someone living with a depressed, pessimistic person is obviously going to be very affected by his mood, as all emotions, both positive and negative, have an infectious quality. To cope with him she will inevitably have to work hard to keep her own attitude optimistic, otherwise she will be drawn down to his low level of awareness where there will be no chance for her to help him let go of his suffering and look at the brighter side of life. She must be very careful not to upset him, as he will be especially vulnerable to negative vibrations.

Signs to look for: handwriting **of any style** that satisfies one or more of these points:

1 Any descending or drooping signature.

David Hamilton   *E. Darwin*

2 Any descending line of writing (make sure you find 3 or more lines that do this).

Sometimes its difficult to think positively

3 Any words that droop downwards (watch for 3 or more words that do this).

The way of least resistance is the best

The Domestic Tyrant

This individual's childhood was probably ruled by a strong-willed, domineering mother. If he has a family of his own, he will attempt to gain control over them in a similar forceful way and will become easily frustrated and irritable if his position of power is questioned. Living with him is obviously going to be very emotionally demanding, and unless his partner is prepared to put up with a great deal of extra conflict she will have to accept him as the boss. He is pedantic and usually places excessively high demands on the members of his family. If they do not live up to his expectations he can be very fault-finding and judgemental, and will frequently manage to make them feel guilty in order to strengthen his control over them. On the positive side, however, he will have highly protective feelings towards them and will work hard to provide a financially secure home. With his forceful personality, leadership, drive and determination, he will inevitably be a good survivor.

Signs to look for: handwriting **of any style** that satisfies one or more of these points:

1 The small letter 'g' or 'y' with a sharply angled triangle **of any shape** (watch for 2 or more triangles like this).

2 The small letter 't' with the crossbar sloping **noticeably** downwards (look for 2 or more 't's where this applies).

3 The small letter 't' where the crossbar forms a star-shape to the left of the stem (you need to see 2 or more 't's with this shape).

The Vain Type

This person places excessive value on his personal appearance, potential qualities, achievements and job success, and feels a strong compulsion to prove both to himself and others that he is a superior being. He has an immense need to gain approval from society and desperately wants to be recognised as a successful and accomplished person. The origin of his neurosis lies in a childhood in which he felt undervalued or rejected in some way: perhaps he considered himself underprivileged in comparison with others or alternatively his parents may have had excessive expectations of him which he felt he would never be able to live up to.

Invariably he will have strong motivation to achieve success in whatever area of work he is involved in, but he needs to be careful that others do not find him affected and conceited. However, because he wants to be accepted, he is likely to have found some way of compensating for the less socially acceptable characteristics associated with such an over-active ego.

He will not be the easiest of people to live with, for his vain nature conceals a troubled mind. His vanity is, in fact, a compensation for feeling inadequate and insecure, as he believes he should be so much more than he really is. Below the superficial layer of superiority, he secretly feels inferior; he grossly undervalues himself, although he does not want others to know this. With some vain people, these inner feelings are rooted so deeply within the subconscious mind that they are unaware of them, mistakenly believing in the thin façade of their own conceit. A person with writing that fits points 2 and/or 3 but not point 1 will tend to conceal their vanity from others to a large extent, so that only those very close to them will be aware of it. But if a person has writing that fits point 1 with or without points 2 and/or 3, then their vanity is likely to be ostentatious and very visible to those they meet.

Signs to look for: handwriting **of any style** that satisfies one or more of these points:

1 Any signature with very large, showy capital letters.

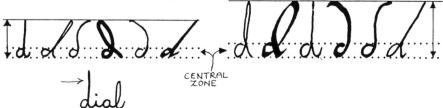

2 The personal pronoun 'I' which is at least 4 times the size of the central zone (look for 2 or more 'I's this size).

3 The small letter 'd' with the stem at least 4 times the size of the central zone (you must find 3 or more 'd's this tall).

The Grudge Bearer

In the past this person had some extremely unpleasant experiences which made him feel bitter and resentful towards a particular person or situation for causing undeserved pain either to himself or to someone he cared about. If the diagonal line mentioned in point 1 starts from far below the base of the letter, then the past experiences responsible for this resentment occurred in his childhood or early teenage years. He may not even realise that they are still affecting him, for they are likely to be festering in his mind below the threshold of his conscious awareness. These pent-up hostile feelings are undoubtedly blocking emotional energy that could be channelled in a more positive direction. He would do well to discuss openly with a sensitive listener any past circumstances which could be the source of his conflicts, for he has developed a marked tendency to bear grudges. When someone has wronged him in some way he will not forgive and forget. He nurtures grievances far too long and has a precise memory for such matters, which can be recalled in detail as vividly as if they had just occurred. His partner should make sure she restrains herself from saying anything nasty to him in the heat of an argument as, even if she did not really mean what she said, he will invariably sulk for an extended period while simultaneously resenting her.

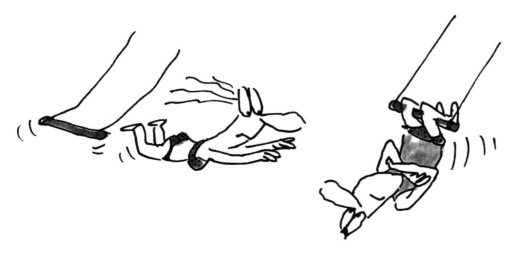

Signs to look for: handwriting **of any style** that satisfies either or both of these points:

1 Capital or small letters beginning with a rigid diagonal line starting from noticeably below the central zone (check for 2 or more letters starting this way).

2 The small letter 'g' or 'y' with a sharply angled triangle that is very noticeably extended to the left (make sure you find 2 or more letters with this kind of triangle).

Sexual Behaviour

Sexual energy is the root of life and mankind has worshipped this energy since time began. The ancient Chinese and Indians, especially, made extensive and refined research into learning how to control, increase and transform it, believing that once this power is correctly harnessed, it can be used to speed up the evolution of consciousness.

The quality of feeling between two people in an intimate relationship is often largely influenced by their level of sexual compatibility – and the excitement felt at the start of a new relationship usually camouflages any potential incompatibility. Partners at this stage are also far more tolerant of one another and are therefore prepared to accept things which could be a source of future conflict. Consequently it is only later in the game, when the romance has cooled a little, that a couple may suddenly discover a large difference between their sexual preferences, and this can lead to considerable tension between them.

By examining handwriting, you can now assess the likely degree of harmony or conflict between the sexual natures of two people.

The Moody Lover

This person has an unpredictable sexual nature ranging from warm and passionate to cold and uninterested. He will be difficult to live with, as his partner will never know where she stands with him. His changeable temperament is a product of a childhood made unhappy by conflict between parents with extremely different and incompatible personalities. His emotions at that time were torn between feelings of love and feelings of strong resentment, and that behaviour pattern still influences him.

Signs to look for: handwriting **of any style** that satisfies this point:

1 Writing in which lines, words or letters **or any combination of these** lean in different directions.

Lines leaning in different directions.

sometimes my emotions seem to control me completely and then at other times I just feel detached from it all.

Words leaning in different directions.

my attitudes change moment to moment

Letters leaning in different directions.

I often feel so inwardly restless

The Sociable Lover

This person thoroughly enjoys meeting and communicating, both in the work sphere and in social life. He has a genuine sensitivity to the state of mind of those he meets, he talks easily and listens well, and people will find him a pleasure to have around. He creates a happy atmosphere.

He will be very dissatisfied if his partner has an unsociable nature and likes her privacy, for he is the type who likes to go out to parties and to be around others in his spare time. If he cannot go out to socialise, he will invariably want to invite people to his own home. Deprive such an individual of an active social life and you are destroying any chance he may have of creating a happy existence for himself.

Signs to look for: handwriting **of any style** that satisfies point 1 **and** one or more of the other points:

1 The small letter 'g' with a smoothly curved balloon appearance. (you need to find 2 or more 'g's like this).

gone gue age bag game green

2 Writing that leans, even slightly, to the right (writing that leans to the right more than the following example is **not** valid).

Understanding feelings is the Key

3 Writing done from choice with a medium or thick felt-tip pen, or any other pen producing broad thick lines.

Relaxation feelings Awareness

4 The capital or small letter 'm' like 2 or 3 joined letter 'i's without dots (watch out for 3 or more 'm's that look like this).

iiet naiiie Mary home my Man

5 The small letter 'd', 'e', 'h', 'm', 'n' or 't' with a cup-shaped ending. The letter must be at the end of a word to be valid (look for 2 or more letters with this ending).

and hid though am can are nut at

The Jealous Lover

This person has underlying feelings of emotional insecurity. Consequently he is extremely possessive and in social situations will keep a sharp lookout for any behaviour on his partner's part which may signal potential infidelity – even the innocent enjoyment of another person's conversation could precipitate jealous feelings. Someone living with a jealous lover obviously needs to be careful if their partner's handwriting also reveals a tendency towards physical aggression, a combination which could have disastrous consequences. In any event, the stability of a relationship will be seriously threatened if either partner's handwriting has the graphological signs for jealousy.

The following description applies predominantly to men: invariably he will be the type who has interrogated his partner fully about the affairs and relationships she had with other men before him and, unless too inhibited to do so, he will have demanded detailed descriptions of those past love-making sessions. He may well torture himself with fears that his body and/or his sexual performance does not equal the standard of previous lovers, and no amount of reassurance from his partner will pacify his mind in this or in other areas of his jealous obsessions.

Psychologists have suggested that neurotic disorders such as the inferiority complex are responsible for jealous behaviour. The root source, however, dates back to the time of our earliest ancestors – this powerful emotion formed a part of Neanderthal society's survival pattern, stimulating whenever necessary a fierce protectiveness that safeguarded tribal members and loved ones from abduction. Unfortunately this emotion is no longer an asset to survival, for it is now incompatible with the more evolved consciousness of modern civilisation. Behaviour connected with the emotion of jealousy is today regarded as an infringement of the personal rights of another individual.

Signs to look for: handwriting **of any style** that satisfies **two** or more of these points:

1 Writing with most of its letters joined together, leaning so far to the right that it appears to be falling over.

emotions having unbearable intensity

trying to control almost uncontrollable impulses

2 Capital or small letters with a hook on the righthand side. Hooks may be large or small (you need to see 4 or more letters with this sign).

T C R J a c d e f h s t y

3 Capital or small letters with a small circular attachment to the beginning of the letter (look for 2 or more letters with this).

Ireland Malta Eva Gone fat sea wit

The Sexual Teaser

This is a predominantly female handwriting characteristic. This person knows just how to manipulate partners into making passes, which she then refuses. When she meets a man she wishes to taunt in this way, she will arouse his passion by flirting so that he really believes she fancies him. She enjoys such games not because she wishes to cause hurt but because she cannot resist testing her allure, and confirming that she is appealing to the opposite sex. Those who have been disappointed by such behaviour would be less upset if they realised that she desperately needs the reassurance and ego-boosting that her flirting and teasing provide.

Signs to look for: handwriting **of any style** that satisfies this point:

1 The small letter 'd' with the stem detached from the round portion (make sure you see 2 or more 'd's where this happens).

The Inhibited Lover

This person is emotionally very repressed. He is extremely secretive about his thoughts and feelings, because he is frightened that if he reveals them to others, they will not accept him. Even his partner may know little of his true inner nature. He is likely to be very self-conscious about his naked body, which he may well hide from his lover when the relationship is new by undressing in the dark. He will be too embarrassed to talk openly about sexual matters and his manner of love-making will be very conventional and lacking in imagination. He is definitely the sort who prefers such activity to be well under the bedclothes.

Signs to look for: handwriting **of any style** that satisfies **both** these points:

1 The small letters 'a' **and** 'o' with an extremely narrow appearance (you need to find 4 **of each** letter like this).

not always around   *is anyone about today?*

2 The small letter 'g' with an extremely narrow appearance. The downstroke may even be retraced by the upstroke (you must see 4 or more 'g's like this).

are you going to go? this gift you gave is great

S e x u a l   P e a c o c k s

Who cares about modesty? These types strut through life confident in the knowledge that they are among the world's sexiest people, and subscribe firmly to the idea that if you've got it, you should flaunt it. Feeling good with themselves, as they generally do, sexual peacocks can be fun to have around: they can start a buzz, or they can spark a day, a party, a person into life. And they honestly believe that they can take that fun straight into bed: they're hot stuff, so no one could possibly emerge from between their sheets, or beneath their duvet, anything but the better for the experience. It could be true, too – but they should take care that this self-confidence doesn't injure others. If their partner overcomes inhibition and takes the lead sometimes, or slows the pace down, it could interrupt the performance of a lifetime and cause quite an upset.

Signs to look for: handwriting **of any style** that satisfies this point:

1 Capital letters extended horizontally. These extended capitals can be joined on to the following letter or not, and they may underline the rest of the word or not (look for 2 or more capitals like this).

Charlie Even Regards Love

The Worried Lover

This person seems to be experiencing feelings of sexual frustration which may stem from a total absence of sex or alternatively he may be dissatisfied with either his own or his partner's sexual performance. He strongly desires really good sex and is worried about how to get it. With so much on his mind he can at times become very restless and uneasy, because even when he stops worrying about these matters at a conscious level, his subconscious simply takes over and continues the process.

Signs to look for: handwriting **of any style** that satisfies this point:

1 The small letter 'a' or 'o' with a line hanging inside the circle (check you find 4 or more letters with this sign).

going on and on one day away

The Unemotional Lover

Few people are fully satisfied with their personality and achievements – self-disapproval seems to be an inherent part of human nature. But in the individual with backward-leaning writing, these feelings are exaggerated to an extreme.

It is likely that the cause of this negative self-concept stems from a childhood in which the person felt rejected or unloved in some way, either in the family or the school environment. Whatever the root of this syndrome, the resultant self-critical attitude has caused him to exert excessive control over his emotions and actions in an effort to conquer his supposed weaknesses, or conceal them from others. His feelings are suppressed and carefully hidden, as he feels he can only trust himself and cannot therefore rely on anyone else. This causes him to live in a state of inner isolation and he will invariably have a deep-rooted sense of loneliness, even when surrounded by family and friends. Because of this sense of separation, he is unlikely to have developed the ability to sense the emotional state of those with whom he communicates, and will instead attempt to use his intellect to deduce what they must be feeling.

He finds little personal fulfilment in relationships or social spheres, so his career tends to dominate his life and he will put all his energy into achieving well in this area. In his leisure time it is very possible that he will seek an outlet for his suppressed emotions, perhaps through books or videos, where he can escape into a fantasy world of romance and adventure. In social encounters he feels tense, self-conscious and mistrustful, and will usually avoid discussing matters of a personal or private nature as he is too insecure of people's reactions. It will be exceptionally difficult, even for highly intuitive and perceptive people, to ascertain what he is really thinking and feeling, as he is at all times a master at maintaining a poker face. Sometimes the social reserve and aloofness of such an individual can be wrongly misinterpreted as snobbishness or conceit.

Occasionally, the person with backward-leaning writing will work extremely hard to compensate for his lack of natural sociability, carefully constructing a well-polished façade to give the false impression that he is a very communicative and friendly human being. His choice of a long-term partner will rarely be determined by a head-over-heels, love at first sight emotional reaction but will instead probably be based upon a careful consideration of hard facts: appearance, social status, financial and family background would be taken into account in order to determine how appropriate the choice is. This individual will undoubtedly not be the easiest of people to live

with. Trying to dissuade him from a particular course of action by appealing to his emotions is liable to prove futile, as he will respond only to reason and solid fact. He will always be inclined to mistrust his partner's love and affection; he has a strong fear of deep emotional involvement and its consequent vulnerability. He is so busy suppressing and controlling his own behaviour that he frequently completely loses awareness of how his partner is feeling and she may therefore consider him somewhat cold and insensitive at times. He is scared of being rejected. He will not easily give sympathy and quite definitely does not like accepting sympathy from others. Because his natural impulses are constantly being held in check, he will be very predictable, as his actions are invariably pre-planned. He will rarely, if ever, demonstrate any spontaneous display of love and affection, for even if he is experiencing such feelings inwardly, he will have great difficulty in expressing them. Living with such a person can at times be very unnerving, as it becomes increasingly difficult to respond in a positive manner to such a reserved, undemonstrative personality.

Male lovers in this category will tend to treat love-making simply as a physical need to be satisfied, as well as an opportunity to confirm to themselves their own virility, in order to boost their ego. Their sexual play, if any, will be stilted and predictable, and without genuine concern for providing sensual gratification to their partner. It is interesting to note that females with backward-leaning writing are quite liable to choose a much older man as a partner, perhaps because of some subconscious desire to achieve the security and protection potentially provided by a father-figure. She will have an unromantic, matter-of-fact attitude to sex, which she will simply view as a necessary part of the relationship which needs to be dealt with. She will tend to expect her partner to make all the moves and will be content to play a somewhat passive role, so that even the most affectionate of lovers will have difficulty in eliciting a romantic response from her. Even if she enjoys love-making, she will nevertheless be in full control of herself and will not suffer any great frustration if deprived of sex, unless she also shows the writing signs of 'The Sexual Athlete' and/or 'The Imaginative Lover'.

Signs to look for: handwriting **of any style** that satisfies this point:

1 Writing that leans to the left as much or more than this:

I prefer to keep my emotions private

inner feelings are difficult to express

achievements rarely live up fully to ones original expectations

The Vocal Casanova

This description applies to men only. This person enjoys creating the impression that he is an experienced lover who knows exactly what it takes to satisfy someone thoroughly in bed. He loves to talk about sex and will gladly relate any previous experience he has had to friends willing to listen. In reality, it is likely that his sexual conquests are considerably less impressive than his conversation suggests, for he spends far more time in talk than in action.

Signs to look for: handwriting **of any style** that satisfies this point:

1 The small letter 'd' with a wide open gap (look for 3 or more 'd's with this gap).

The Imaginative Lover

For men:

The images which pass through the mind of this person would be an inspiration to any erotic film producer or author of naughty books. It has been discovered that men become temporarily impotent when they are imprisoned for years in solitary confinement without any sexual relationship; but this individual could come out of such an ordeal with his virility still well intact because his erotic fantasy is so powerful that to him, his imaginary, voluptuous bedfellows become reality. His vivid imaginings have a potentially negative side-effect, however, for there is a grave danger that the sexual experiences he has in real life will not come anywhere near the quality of those that exist in his mind. Indeed, the comparison can be bitterly disappointing, and leave him with feelings of immense sexual frustration. There is fortunately an effective antidote to this possible problem. If he can find a lover with an erotic fantasy matching his own, they could achieve great sexual harmony and satisfaction together by indulging themselves in a wide variety of sexual games and innovative love-making positions.

For women:

This person's fantasies will be very different from those of her male counterpart. Male sexual imagery is usually somewhat primitive and focuses mainly on variations of the sexual act, excluding the more emotional aspects of love-making. A woman's fantasies are considerably more romantic. Tender courtship rituals will usually be visualised prior to any sexual imagery, and when the erotic part of her fantasising does begin you can be sure it will include an abundance of touching plus loving foreplay. Only then is she likely to reach the point where she fantasises about sexual intercourse and its variations. She would be considered by most men to be an extremely satisfying lover but unfortunately it will be very difficult for her to find someone to satisfy her own needs. She will quickly tire of any lover who has routine love-making patterns, for not only does she need her partner to be sexually spontaneous and inventive, but in addition she requires someone who has an essentially romantic nature.

Signs to look for: handwriting **of any style** that satisfies this point:

1 The small letter 'g' with an over-inflated balloon appearance **of any shape** (make sure you find 3 or more 'g's that look like this).

The Frustrated Lover

There are several possible causes of this condition. It may be that he is still not fully matured emotionally and therefore has not reached his full potential to enjoy sex. Alternatively, it is possible that he has no current partner. A third possibility is that he is involved with someone too inhibited to make love in a satisfying manner, or simply not interested in making love as often as he is. Lastly, he may be having personal problems which make him too tense to relax in love-making.

Signs to look for: handwriting **of any style** that satisfies this point:

1 The small letter 'g' with an ascending line that nearly always fails to reach the central zone.

CENTRAL ZONE

Genital Fixation

This description applies to men only except in extremely rare cases. This person is obsessed with his genitalia and cannot help thinking about them from morning till night. Even when he sleeps he is unlikely to escape his problem, due to frequent erotic dreams. It is possible that his fixation stems from early childhood when he developed guilt feelings about sexual arousal. Attempts to suppress his natural sexual nature caused his subconscious to produce instead this unnatural obsession with the sexual organs.

Signs to look for: handwriting **of any style** that satisfies this point:

1 The capital letter 'C' with any type of curled hook. The hook must be in the top part of the letter to be valid (look for 2 or more 'C's like this).

The Considerate Lover

This person has a flexible sexual nature. His sensitivity to other people's needs allows him to alter his approach in order to satisfy a wide range of different sexual appetites. Because he has an air of self-assurance in this area of life, he will be able to make even shy and inexperienced lovers feel at ease and can comfortably initiate them into a wider appreciation of the pleasure of sex.

Signs to look for: handwriting **of any style** that satisfies point 1, **and** one or more of the other points:

1 The small letter 'g' with a smoothly curved balloon-shaped appearance (look for 4 or more 'g's like this).

gone give age bag game green

2 The small letter 'd' or 't' with a looped stem (you must identify 4 or more of this type of stem).

and rod bed dog doing too at mat eat

3 The small letter 'd', 'e', 'h', 'm', 'n' or 't' with a cup-shaped ending. The letter must be at the end of a word to be valid (you need to spot 4 or more letters like this).

and hid though am can are nut at

4 The capital letter 'K' where the arms form a loop round the stem (be sure you see 2 or more 'K's with this sign).

K K K K

5 Writing that leans, even slightly, to the right (writing that leans to the right more than the following example is **not** valid).

Understanding feelings is the Key

The Sexual Bully

For men:

This person has an extremely assertive, headstrong nature and always strives to get his way. In an intimate relationship his behaviour will be tyrannical: he will expect and push his partner to comply with his wishes. If she does not, he will become irritable and will attack the vulnerable spots in her ego in order to weaken her self-esteem and drive her into submission. His sexual desires are strong and he will become easily frustrated if he is deprived of what he considers to be his rights. It is possible that he may even use his physical strength to encourage his partner to succumb to him. On the other hand, he will inevitably be an excellent survivor and a good provider of material security, as he has an abundance of natural fighting spirit.

For women:

This person will be the boss of the household and will make sure that her man does what he is told. She is likely to be very dissatisfied with her partner's personality and could well be a classic example of the nagging wife.

Signs to look for: handwriting **of any style** that satisfies one or more of these points:

1 The small letter 'g' or 'y' with a sharply angled triangle **of any shape** (watch for 2 or more triangles like this).

2 The small letter 't' with the crossbar sloping **noticeably** downwards (look for 4 or more 't's where this applies).

3 The small letter 't' with a crossbar that **noticeably** thickens on one side (you need to find 2 or more 't's where this happens).

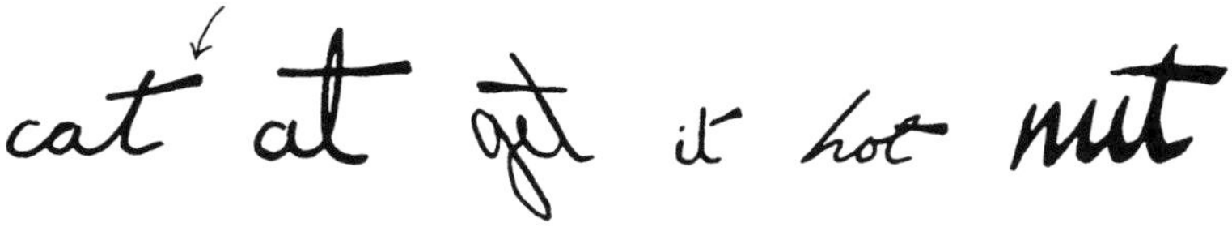

The Self-conscious Lover

What others think of this person's appearance and behaviour is of prime importance to him. In the area of love-making, therefore, he will need plenty of praise and reassurance as without this he will automatically feel his performance has been inadequate. His sensitive nature is easily hurt by criticism, but he responds specially well to compliments, which he will return in a warm, loving way. If his partner puts him down, however, he will not easily forget.

Signs to look for: handwriting **of any style** that satisfies either or both of these points:

1 The small letter 'd' with a tall looped stem that is at least 4 times the size of the central zone (look for 2 or more 'd's with this size of stem).

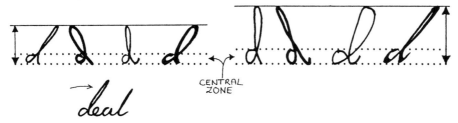

CENTRAL ZONE

deal

2 The small letter 'm' with **rounded** tops, the last of which is **noticeably** taller (check you find 2 or more 'm's like this).

more man frame drama aim

The Apathetic Lover

In a woman's handwriting, this graphological sign will not always mean that she is a boring lover, for it could well indicate someone who is not having any sex life whatsoever. She may be fully involved with her career and/or family and have no real interest in or need for sex. Alternatively, if she is involved in a sexual relationship, it will mean that she has a very matter-of-fact, unemotional attitude towards sex. She derives little real pleasure from it, and her partner is likely to feel frustrated with her lack of warmth and excitement, unless he has the same nature.

In a man's writing this reveals a person who is most probably channelling so much energy into his career that he has little left for sexual relationships. Consequently he derives only a small portion of the pleasure potentially available from love-making. Sex has become for him merely a routine release from the pressures of daily work. He will have little interest in the niceties of courtship and foreplay. His partner will invariably consider his love-making somewhat monotonous and unexciting. Unfortunately things will not alter until he decides to place a little less value on career success, and a little more value on sensual enjoyment.

Signs to look for: handwriting **of any style** that satisfies this point:

1 The small letter 'g' that nearly always has just a straight descending line.

gone bag hug dig get green

The Hugger Lover

This person craves and needs plenty of affection, the sort who with a willing partner will frequently engage in touching, stroking and hugging. For him there is no substitute for a really good cuddle and no matter how satisfying love-making may be, when it is finished he will never willingly neglect the opportunity to lie in his partner's warm embrace and drift off to sleep. In his childhood he is unlikely to have received sufficient parental affection and as an adult is searching to escape the emotional insecurity that this caused. It will be deeply distressing for such a person if he is with someone who cannot give him the warmth of human contact he so desperately needs.

Signs to look for: handwriting **of any style** that satisfies this point:

1 The capital letter 'K' where the arms form either a loop or a half-circle and only **lightly touch** the stem. Examples where the arms pass through the stem are not valid (look for 2 or more 'K's with this sign).

The Nervous Lover

For some reason this individual seems to have an underlying fear of the sexual act. He will thoroughly enjoy giving and receiving affection and could well be the sort who fully appreciates a loving cuddle, but when it comes to intimate foreplay leading up to intercourse he begins to freeze and will feel embarrassment and general uneasiness. Anyone beginning an intimate relationship with this person would be well advised to proceed slowly, giving encouragement and reassurance.

Signs to look for: handwriting **of any style** that satisfies this point:

1 The capital letter 'K' or 'R' with the arms detached from the stem (you need to see 2 or more letters where this happens).

The Sensual Lover

This person is ruled by his very strong, instinctive, earthy nature, and is able to enjoy to the full all the pleasures of life. He is turned on far more than most by the delicate taste of fine food and wine, and will seek out any opportunity to stimulate his senses to their maximum. The courtship ritual will inevitably include a night out at a fine restaurant, with soft lights and beautiful music, and there is every possibility that on arriving at his home he will prepare a warm scented bath for two, filled with bubbles.

His sexual feelings are easily aroused and he will not hesitate to touch, caress and explore his partner's body, inebriated by her unique sexual aroma: most definitely a pheromone connoisseur. His choice of holiday is very unlikely to be a trip entailing endless and exhausting sight-seeing; he would far rather lie stretched out on a soft, sandy beach, soaking up the warm rays of the sun and titillating his senses with gentle dips into clear, cool water. It should come as no surprise to learn that this individual is likely to tire quickly of any partner who does not share his taste for the good life; note that if provoked, anyone of this nature whose handwriting includes the graphological sign described in point 1, denoting a strong force of animal instinct, could occasionally express anger physically.

Signs to look for: handwriting **of any style** that satisfies one or more of these points:

1 Any letters clogged with ink (look for 3 or more letters where this happens).

what is that Come back look at it

2 Writing with many words heavily crossed out.

I was ~~~~ going along   I believe ~~~~ we can

3 Writing done from choice with a medium or thick felt-tip pen, or any other pen producing broad thick lines.

Relaxation feelings Awareness

4 Writing with a messy appearance caused by smudges and blotches made by the pen.

5 Writing where heavy pen pressure makes indentations that clearly show on the reverse of the paper.

The Fault-finding Lover

This person will expect his partner to conform closely to his own standards of behaviour and will be extremely annoyed if she fails to do so. He has a very low tolerance of people who, in his opinion, do not behave correctly and he misuses his sharp, analytical mind for the purpose of judging them. His rigid outlook makes him stubbornly convinced that he is always right – don't expect him to compromise. Satisfaction is gained from pointing out his partner's faults in an insensitive and unpleasant manner. In arguments, he will not hesitate to bring up her past errors and will use these, and any other criticisms he can find, as evidence of her imperfection.

This will inevitably damage her self-esteem and confidence. Indeed, this is the subconscious intention behind the fault-finder's actions. He is extremely critical of himself, even if this is not evident. Believing he should be far more than he is, and seeking to relieve the pain caused by this negative assessment, he attempts to diminish his partner's worth so that he, in comparison, will seem to be better. This behaviour is a probable consequence of frequent criticism received from parents during childhood. It is also likely that their expectations of him were excessively high and virtually impossible to satisfy.

The following description applies only to men: he could well be the type who criticises his partner's physical appearance, if he feels it is below standard. Alternatively, he may nag about domestic inefficiency, social slip-ups or sexual performance.

Signs to look for: handwriting **of any style** that satisfies one or more of these 3 main points:

1 One or more of the following letter shapes, each appearing in the writing at least twice:

The capital letter 'M' beginning with a sharply angled peak that rises noticeably above the rest of the letter.

Capital or small letters with a final line rising noticeably higher and curving to the right.

The small letter 'g' or 'y' with a sharply angled triangle of any shape.

The small letter 't' with a crossbar that **noticeably** thickens on one side.

The small letter 't' with the crossbar sloping **noticeably** downwards.

2 Two or more of the following letter shapes appearing in the writing at least twice:

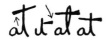

The small letter 'm' or 'n' shaped like a shark's tooth.

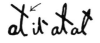

The small letter 'd' or 't' with an ending that descends noticeably below the base of the letter.

2 continued

and at it

The small letter 'd' or 't' with a sharply angled diagonally ascending ending. The letter must be at the end of the word to be valid.

dog ats

The small letter 'd' or 't' with a part that curls under like an eagle's talon.

put it

The small letter 't' with the crossbar on the right, detached from the stem.

T too

The capital or small letter 't' with a crossbar that has sharply angled hooks on both sides.

nut

The small letter 't' where the crossbar forms a star-shape to the left of the stem.

Tom met

The capital or small letter 't' with the crossbar sharp like a needlepoint on either side.

q yq y

The small letter 'g' or 'y' with a very firm and straight descending line that is **noticeably** blunt at the end.

g y

The small letter 'g' or 'y' with a descending line that becomes sharp like a needlepoint at the end.

g yg y

The small letter 'g' or 'y' which is sharply angled at the bottom of the stem.

3 The small letters 'h', 'm' **and** 'n' sharply angled at the top and bottom (you need to find 4 or more **of each** letter).

mahogany WUMAM handsome

The Book Lover

This individual will not feel his leisure hours are wasted if he curls up on a comfortable sofa or bed with some really stimulating reading material. If his lifestyle allows him, he will undoubtedly be an avid reader. This will at times be a source of irritation to his partner, who will have great difficulty in arousing his sexual passion when he is engrossed in an exciting book. Happily, there is an ideal solution. Supply him with erotic literature: although he may find this compelling reading, sooner or later theory is bound to lead to practice.

Signs to look for: handwriting **of any style** that satisfies either or both of these points:

1 The small letter 'd' where the stem is a single ascending line curving to the left (look for 4 or more 'd's like this).

dog grade day dim lic mud

2 The capital or small letter 'e' looking like a backward-facing number 3 (you need to spot 4 or more 'e's like this).

Edna egg meal Easy pet End

The Resentful Lover

Some distant past event has left this person with strong feelings of resentment towards a specific member of the opposite sex he feels was responsible for harming him in some way. He felt frustrated at the time because he believed this individual escaped richly deserved punishment. Unable to do anything about it and incapable of coming to terms with this frustration, he repressed these negative feelings in his subconscious where they have fermented over the years. These blocked emotions have precipitated an attitude of generalised contempt for the opposite sex. This can cause him to behave in an antagonistic manner towards his partner, who becomes a scapegoat for the unexpressed hostility.

Signs to look for: handwriting **of any style** that satisfies this point:

1 The capital letter 'K' or 'R' where the arms form a sharp angle piercing the stem (make sure you find 2 or more letters where this happens).

The Offbeat Lover

Conventional ways of love-making are of no interest to this person. He cannot seem to derive any real excitement from sex unless it involves unorthodox practices. He has a vivid, erotic fantasy and his mind is filled with images of himself gaining sexual pleasure in ways which would be described by most people as somewhat unacceptable. Anyone intending to begin an intimate relationship with this person should therefore find out first exactly what his sexual tastes are or they could be in for an unpleasant surprise, unless their own desires are similar.

Signs to look for: handwriting **of any style** that satisfies either or both of these points:

❶ Capital or small letters with any type of phallus-shaped appearance or protrusion (look for 2 or more letters with this sign).

❷ The small letter 'g' that has an extremely strange shape of any sort (you need to see 2 or more 'g's like this).

The Self-centred Lover

This person is obsessed with himself and the way life is treating him, to such an extent that in an intimate relationship he may have little energy left for caring effectively about his partner. He has an exaggerated sense of his own importance which makes him over-react when faced with misfortune or mistreatment. Because he occupies such an over-sized portion of his own sphere of awareness, he cannot help diminishing the value he places upon the existence of those around him. His partner is likely to find him very egocentric and inattentive to her personal needs.

The following description applies predominantly to men and only rarely to women: he will tend to dominate an excessively large part of any conversation with his own opinions and experiences, leaving little time or space for his partner to express herself. Even when he does listen, she will sense that he is not really tuning in to her wavelength, as his mind will be constantly focused on thoughts about himself. His relationships will be doomed to failure unless he improves this side of his personality, since effective communication is an indispensable foundation stone of compatibility.

Signs to look for: handwriting **of any style** that satisfies one or more of these points:

1 Capital letters in handwriting or signature that are very large **and** showy (look for 2 or more capitals like this).

2 Any personal pronoun 'I' that is at least 4 times the size of the central zone (check you find 2 or more 'I's this size).

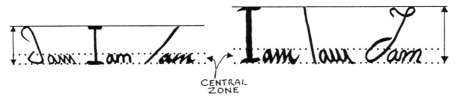

3 Handwriting where the central zone is as large or larger than this:

The Sexual Athlete

For men:

This person's sexual energy is unusually strong and he is subject to feelings of arousal far more frequently than the average person. He possesses plenty of natural physical stamina and is likely to be ambitious and hard working, but no matter how involved he may become with his job he will never show any signs of a decreasing interest in sex, which will always hold an extremely high position in his life's value system.

As a partner, he is bound to be considered extremely demanding unless his lover has an equal sexual appetite. Not only will he desire sex on a daily basis but he will quickly recover his energy and want at least one repeat performance, for he is without doubt a natural sexual athlete – the perfect companion for over-sexed lovers. The drawback to possessing such a strong sexual nature is that he will experience extreme frustration when deprived of what he considers sufficient sex. If things do not change he will become very depressed with his life, as it will seem that the very foundations of his existence are threatened. He will therefore be unable to find any real happiness if his long-term partner's sex drive is low, and if she denies him sex too frequently there is a good chance that he will be tempted to look elsewhere. Even if he has a faithful nature, his powerful sexual instinct could well override the conscious self-control mechanism of his intellect, and he is likely to succumb when temptation presents itself, no matter how guilty he may feel about it. However, infidelity in this case is almost forgivable, because the forces of Nature have an iron grip on this particular member of the human species.

For women:

Cultural conditioning may well have resulted in a suppression of this person's natural impulse to exercise their abundance of sexual energy. Many societies have hypocritical double standards for men and women with regard to sexual behaviour: if a woman plays the Casanova game, she is liable to be unfairly branded as immoral or, alternatively, to be labelled a nymphomaniac. Consequently, many females in this category choose to sublimate their sexuality through work or some other channel.

Signs to look for: handwriting **of any style** that satisfies either or both of these points:

1 The small letter 'g' with a descending line at least 3½ times the size of the central zone (look for 3 or more 'g's where this applies).

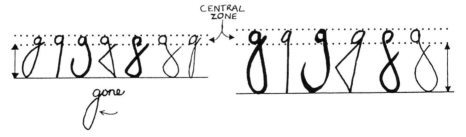

2 The small letter 'g' with an over-inflated balloon appearance **of any shape** in writing where heavy pen pressure makes indentations that clearly show on the reverse of the paper (you need to see 2 or more 'g's like this).

Acknowledgements

A very special thank you to Charles Cole for all the knowledge, inspiration and personal supervision given to me when I began my study of graphology many years ago. In addition, my appreciation to Dorothy Hodos for her help during those early years.

Also, gratitude to the late Geri Stuparich.

Finally, I would like to thank my family for their continued support and encouragement, and most of all, my wife Iwona.

Bibliography

Cole, Charles — *Handwriting Analysis Workshop Unlimited Basics* (private publication)

Currer-Briggs, Noel, Brian Kennet and Jane Patterson — *Handwriting Analysis in Business – The Use of Graphology in Personnel Selection*, Associated Business Programmes, 1971

Falcon, Hal, Ph.D. — *How to Analyse Handwriting*, Trident Press, 1964

Hartford, Huntington — *You Are What You Write*, Macmillan Publishing Company, Inc., 1973

Jacoby, H. J. — *Self-Knowledge Through Handwriting*, J. M. Dent and Sons, Ltd., 1941

Klages, Dr Ludwig — *Handschrift und Charakter*, Verlag Von Johann Ambrosius Barth, 1921

Le Guen, Monique — *Graphology*, Media Books, 1976

Marcuse, Irene, Ph.D. — *Guide to Personality Through Your Handwriting*, Arco Publishing Company, Inc., 1974

Mendel, A. O. — *Personality in Handwriting – A Handbook of American Graphology*, Stephen Daye Press, 1947

Meyer, Jerome S. — *The Handwriting Analyser*, Simon & Schuster, 1974

Olyanova, Nadya — *Handwriting Tells*, Wilshire Book Company, 1973

———— — *The Psychology of Handwriting – Secrets of Handwriting Analysis*, Wilshire Book Company, 1973

Paterson, Jane — *Interpreting Handwriting*, David McKay Company, Inc., 1976

Pulver, Max — *Symbolism of Handwriting*, Orell Fussli Verlag, 1931

Roman, Klara, Ph.D. — *The Encyclopaedia of the Written Word – A Lexicon for Graphology and Other Aspects of Writing*, Frederick Ungor Publishing Company, 1968

———— — *Handwriting, A Key to Personality*, Noonday Press, 1952

Rosen, Billie Pesin — *The Science of Handwriting Analysis – A Guide to Character and Personality*, Paperback Library, Inc., 1968

Saudek, Robert — *The Psychology of Handwriting*, George Allen and Unwin, Ltd., 1925

Sonnemann, Ulrich, Ph.D. — *Handwriting Analysis as a Psychodiagnostic Tool*, Grune and Stratton, Inc., 1950

Victor, Frank, Ph.D. — *Handwriting, A Personality Projection*, Charles C. Thomas, 1952

Wolff, Werner, Ph.D. — *Diagrams of the Unconscious – Handwriting and Personality in Measurement, Experiment and Analysis*, Grune and Stratton, Inc., 1948

INDEX

Capital and small letters

Size of writing

Very small writing. Any style of writing with a central zone as small or smaller than this is valid   **10, 21, 39, 47**

Very large writing. Any style of writing with a central zone as large or larger than this is valid   **12, 15, 19, 49, 139**

Words with letters diminishing in height without loss of legibility   **63**

Style of writing

Any writing leaning right   **65, 107, 123**

Any writing leaning so far right it looks as if falling over   **93, 109**

Any writing leaning far left   **116**

Any writing with lines, words or letters leaning in different directions   **105**

Any ascending lines of writing   **71**

Any descending lines of writing   **97**

Signatures